TALES OF THE GURKHAS

Harold James is the co-author (with Denis Sheil-Small) of:

The Gurkhas (Macdonald 1965)
The Undeclared War (Leo Cooper 1971)
A Pride of Gurkhas (Leo Cooper 1975)

TALES OF THE GURKHAS

Harold James

The Book Guild Ltd
Sussex, England

The Book Guild Ltd,
25 High Street,
Lewes, Sussex.

First published 1991
© Harold James 1991
Set in Baskerville
Typesetting by Southern Reproductions (Sussex)
East Grinstead, Sussex
Printed in Great Britain by
Antony Rowe Ltd.
Chippenham, Wiltshire.

British Library Cataloguing in Publication Data
James, Harold 1923 –
    Tales of the Gurkhas
    I. Title
    823.914 [F]

ISBN 0 86332 555 6

In Memory of:
My Mother, for many years of encouragement.
And Norman and Joey who made it possible.

PRAYER FOR THE GURKHA

O God, who in the Gurkha has given to mankind a race exceptional in courage and devotion, resplendent in its cheerfulness, we, who owe so much, ask Your special blessing on them, their families and their land. Grant us Thy Grace to be loyal to their best interests, as they have been to ours in the past.

(Part of the Gurkha Brigade Association Annual Reunion Service, held in the Royal Memorial Chapel, RMA, Sandhurst.)

CONTENTS

Some Small Items Of Evidence

It had been a long, hard and bloody fighting patrol, and Jemadar Nandabahadur Thapa was relieved to be back within the battalion's perimeter with only one man dead and two wounded. When he reported to the Intelligence Officer he felt tired but sustained by pride in his men who had put up such a good fight.

'How many Japanese did your patrol account for?' asked the IO, a prim young man who was meticulous in carrying out his duties according to the rules and regulations.

'At least five, Sahib. And probably a good few more.'

'Have you any evidence to support your claim?'

Nandabahadur was perplexed for a moment. The old IO had never queried his word. 'I have my second-in-command,' he suggested at last.

The IO smiled in a superior way. 'I meant some concrete evidence such as documents, equipment – well, it might be difficult to bring back all the equipment, but some small items would suffice.'

'Some small items,' Nandabahadur repeated, a gleam in his hard brown eyes which the British officers who knew him well would have recognised, but which escaped this new arrival to the battalion.

A short while later Nandabahadur returned from another highly successful patrol, and once again the IO asked him how many of the enemy had been killed.

'Ten, Sahib,' the Gurkha said.

The IO looked incredulous. 'I told you about evidence. . .' he began.

Nandabahadur interrupted him. 'Yes, Sahib. Small items of Japanese equipment.'

He opened his haversack, and with a broad grin emptied its

contents onto the table.

The Intelligence Officer pushed back his chair and jumped to his feet in horror at the sight of ten pairs of ears.

The Basketball Bomber

They still talk about the Long Man in the regiment. *The Lamo Sahib,* the Gurkhas called him. He was six feet five inches tall, well-built in proportion, with rugged but not unpleasant features and a mop of black, unruly hair. His name was Andrew Miller, and he joined the regiment in 1944 – the penultimate year of the war against Japan.

When the jeep, bringing Andrew from the railway station pulled up outside the headquarters of the 4th Battalion, 15th Gurkha Rifles, Jitbahadur Gurung glanced casually out of his office window. The little jemadar adjutant did not look with great interest as new officers were always arriving in wartime. But as this new officer uncoiled himself from the passenger seat, Jitbahadur leapt to his feet as though it were the Festival of Lights and someone had let off a firework under his chair.

'Ayee–ee!' he cried out, startling the adjutant's clerks by his untypical show of emotion. And they, too, looked out of the window.

Second-Lieutenant Miller, unaware of the excitement his arrival had caused, took two giant steps towards the battalion's administrative office, bowing his head to enter the front door. Meanwhile, Jitbahadur slipped out of the building and marched smartly to C Company lines where he found Havildar Tekbir Gurung.

'Did you see the new officer?' the jemadar asked.

Tekbir shrugged his shoulders. 'If you have seen one you have seen them all,' he muttered.

'Then you have obviously not seen him.'

'Why, what is so wonderful about him, Jemadar Sahib?'

'He must be at least six feet six inches tall,' Jitbahadur explained.

'Ah!' The havildar nodded his head knowingly. But to keep up his reputation as an obstinate and pessimistic man, he added. 'Perhaps he cannot play basketball.'

'In that case we will teach him,' said Jitbahadur determinately. As captain of the battalion's basketball team, nothing was going to deflate his moment of excitement.

For several years the Indian Army Basketball Championship had been a vital contest between the 15th and their deadly rivals, the 12th Punjab Rangers. Humiliatingly the 12th were well ahead on wins because the members of their team were much taller; the arrival of the gigantic new officer seemed to offer a great chance for revenge in what could be the last championship for some time, for the battalion's posting to the war in Burma was imminent.

☆ ☆ ☆

So it was that within a couple of days, Andrew found himself on the battalion basketball pitch in shorts, singlet and canvas shoes. He was nineteen, only a week out of Bangalore Officers' Training School, and very nervous. His commission into the Gurkhas had caused great amusement. 'How on earth will you be able to keep in step?' pointed out one officer cadet. 'Those little Gurkhas' legs go up and down like pistons when they are marching.'

Andrew had been filled with foreboding at the prospect, yet here was the jemadar adjutant of the 4/15th Gurkhas welcoming him as though he had been specially selected for the regiment.

'I understand that the Sahib has not played this game?' queried Jitbahadur in Gurkhali.

Andrew could not speak the Gurkhas' language so Captain Carter, who was there to interpret, confirmed that the young officer was a beginner.

The jemadar adjutant cast an eye over Andrew, and was thankful to note that he was, at least, in good physical shape. 'Very well, Sahib,' said Jitbahadur. 'Let us see how good you are at ball control.'

Havildar Tekbir Gurung, who had been idling in the background bouncing a basketball, suddenly flicked a pass and Andrew took it in the midriff. The havildar retrieved the ball with a derisive smile, but Jitbahadur said cuttingly, 'Wait till the Sahib is ready next time. Remember, he is only a beginner.'

Tekbir lobbed the ball slowly to Andrew who let it slip through his hands. Carter turned away and groaned softly, and the havildar sneered openly. Even Jitbahadur's cheerful, moonface waned – but only for a moment.

'Well, Sahib,' he said easily. 'We obviously have a lot of hard training ahead of us, but I can tell that you have a natural talent.'

Oh, ten out of ten, Jemadar Sahib! said Carter to himself before he translated Jitbahadur's words for Andrew. Tekbir choked as though on a bone. But the little jemadar bustled along, explaining the rules, and finally arranging a demonstration match.

Andrew who had steadily grown more nervous and embarrassed, felt even worse as he watched the men bounce the ball about, manoeuvre trickily, slip guards, pass with perfect precision and shoot the ball accurately into the net. I'll never do it, he thought, miserably.

But he did not allow for Jitbahadur's tenacity, nor the fact that he himself had hidden depths of determination and grit, and above all a friendly nature which earned him the Gurkhas' respect and affection. He was soon being called *The Lamo Sahib*.

For several weeks everyone in the battalion, from the CO, Lieutenant-Colonel Talbot, to the most junior rifleman, watched Andrew's progress with keen interest as he played in practice game after practice game. He gradually developed into an effective player, but Jitbahadur did not include him in the preliminary games of the championships but waited until the semi-finals which the 15th won fairly comfortably, Andrew scoring four goals. Jitbahadur was now reasonably happy to gamble *The Lamo Sahib* in the final. Havildar Tekbir, however, was still not convinced and forecast disaster.

In the Officers' Mess, on the eve of the final, excitement was running high, and heavy bets were laid with the quartermaster who had opened a book.

'You stand to lose a fortune if we win, Quartermaster,' the CO pointed out.

'No, I'm covered, Colonel. The Rangers have placed their

bets with me as well. And of course Brigade all favour the Rangers.'

The colonel saw that Andrew was in earshot. 'Now don't you worry, Miller,' he said quickly. 'Our money is on you, but it doesn't really matter a damn if we should lose. After all, you've done wonders in the past – what is it? – five weeks or so.'

'It's kind of you to say so, sir,' said Andrew, but he knew that the colonel would mind. His stomach felt as though it were tied up in enough knots to test Houdini, and after dinner, for which he had no appetite, he went to bed early.

He lay on his *charpoy*, looking up at the Indian cloth ceiling and dreading the following day. He thought he would never fall asleep, but suddenly it was morning and his orderly came in with a large mug of steaming tea.

Andrew sat on the edge of the bed, sipping the tea slowly. Then he stepped out onto the verandah, shivering for a moment in the unexpected cool of the Indian dawn. The heat would come soon enough but now the air was refreshing. The dust lay undisturbed and the slowly rising sun was tinging the banyan and the distant tamarinds a soft gold.

He knew that this was to be a day to remember – hopefully with pride but perhaps with shame.

The big match was to take place on the Garrison Sports Ground where the basketball pitch was in the open, with no seating for spectators except for a few rows of chairs reserved for officers. And in the early evening, when the temperature had dropped to a more bearable degree, lorry loads of Gurkhas and Punjabis converged on it, cheering and calling out friendly abuse. They soon formed a thick mass around the pitch, chattering, whistling, laughing as some joker shouted out a crude remark.

The officers gradually filled up the special chairs to the accompaniment of catcalls from soldiers brave in the anonymity of the crowd.

The Gurkha team was first out onto the pitch, Andrew towering above Jitbahadur and Tekbir, and the other two Gurkhas, Manbahadur and Ranjit. But when the 12th Punjab Rangers followed shortly, the shouts and laughter suddenly died away into an uncanny silence. The Rangers also had a

14

new team member, a British officer every inch as tall as *The Lamo Sahib* but a few years older, with fair hair and moustache. The way he nonchalantly bounced the ball as though it were a part of his hand told its own story.

Quickly as the silence came then it was broken as the Punjabis roared their pleasure and the Gurkhas chattered anxiously. Lieutenant-Colonel Talbot leaned across to his opposite number in the Rangers. 'I see, Roger, that you have made a change in your team,' he said.

The Rangers' colonel smiled, 'Captain Greenacres. Yes, he's been on secondment as an instructor, but reported back yesterday for our move to Burma. Couldn't go to war without Greenacres, you know.'

'He seems to have arrived at a very opportune moment.'

'As you say, Charles – and he's a very good player. I notice you've also got a new team member . . .'

In the 15th Gurkhas' team there was already consternation. 'I told you so,' said Tekbir.

'Shut up!' Jitbahadur snapped. 'We will still win.'

For Andrew the next five minutes were the worst he had ever experienced. From the time the referee's whistle started the game the Rangers were all over the Gurkhas. Andrew played as though he had never seen a basketball before, muffing passes, allowing Greenacres to out-jump him and trick him. His collapse affected the rest of the team and in a few minutes the Rangers were ten goals up.

Talbot sat very still, ashen beneath his sunburn. Captain Carter wanted to look away, but like a monkey petrified by a python he was unable to do so. The Gurkha supporters were almost silent; and the Punjabis scenting certain victory were shouting their heads off with joy. The game would have ended in a rout if Greenacres had not made what was a really stupid tactical error. He had the ball and Andrew was facing him nervously, wondering which way he would turn. Their faces were close together as Greenacres said, 'Always thought you Gurkha chaps were a lot of poofs. No bloody backbone.'

Looking into the sneering blue eyes Andrew felt a jolt to his system. He did not realize that this was a turning point in his life. All he experienced was a great anger soaring through his whole body and yet his mind was icily controlled. He knew instinctively which way Greenacres was going to pass, and intercepting with perfect timing took the ball, bounced it forward, wrong-footed another Ranger, then rose like a rocket to drop it into the net. The roar of cheering from the Gurkha ranks beat about his head like great waves.

From then on he played skilfully, inspiring his team until by half-time the score stood at Rangers twenty-eight, Gurkhas twenty. As they sucked their lemons in the short interval, he talked tactics. In the past weeks he had picked up quite a good working knowledge of the language and so he was able to encourage his team. Jitbahadur was delighted; *The Lamo Sahib* had grown up and learned the meaning of authority. It was as it should be. No matter what happened in the second half he believed that they had already achieved a small triumph.

As Greenacres and Andrew stood waiting at the centre tap for the start of the second half there was a complete difference in their attitudes. Greenacres's eyes were no longer sardonic – if anything, Andrew decided, there was a hint of doubt in them, but not fear. Greenacres was not a man to frighten easily, but certainly he must be wondering if his side would win as convincingly as he had at first believed.

The referee threw in the ball, and play began in a second half which was to go down as the best ever seen at the Army Championship. The passing, the shooting, the tactics were fast and accurate, and the battle went first one way, then another, until the scores were level at sixty.

With only seconds remaining, a draw seemed inevitable, but in the dying moments Tekbir launched an attack, racing down the middle, bouncing the ball, with Manbahadur and Ranjit wide on his flanks. Then Jitbahadur came up, Tekbir made as though to pass. But as the Ranger marking him fell for the ploy, Tekbir turned on the balls of his feet and threw the ball to Andrew coming up suddenly on the other side.

He took the pass, made a couple of bounces, and soared up towards the net. Greenacres had anticipated a little late, but made a great effort to jump with Andrew and put him off his shot. It seemed to everyone watching as if the two huge men were suspended in mid-air, then Andrew's hand went over Greenacres's desperately clutching fingers and the ball fell through the ring into the net. A brief moment later the referee blew his whistle for time.

The winning of the Indian Army Basketball Championship, and the news that the battalion was to move up to the Burma front, called for an immediate celebration. So this double occasion was marked by a memorable *nautch.*

On the parade ground, the British and Gurkha officers sat at a long trestle table, facing the dancers and the musicians, while spread out in a huge half circle behind the dancers were the other ranks of the battalion, wild with excitement.

Andrew sat between the jemadar adjutant and Subedar-Major Ganje Thapa – a great honour, because the subedar-major did not bestow his patronage lightly, especially to a newly-joined second-lieutenant. Andrew felt himself growing more and more tipsy, which he could not understand as his glass never seemed to get empty. The secret was an old ploy of Gurkha officers. While Jitbahadur attracted Andrew's attention in conversation, the subedar-major would fill up the glass with rum. When Andrew had taken a drink or two, Ganje would distract his attention while Jitbahadur replenished the glass.

The drummers beat out a fast rhythm on their *madals* as the *nautch* dancers whirled on their bare feet, ankle bells jingling, arms and hands moving with snake-like grace, depicting their story of the song. Because Gurkha women do not usually dance in public, female impersonators often take their place. In the battalion the young Gurkha soldiers dressed in female attire were called *marunis,* while their partners, in male Nepalese costume, were *pursengis.*

One of the *marunis* approached the officers' table and seductively invited Andrew to join the dance. A huge shout of *'Lamo Sahib! Lamo Sahib!'* resounded around the ground, interspersed with shrill whistles, and there was much hilarity as Andrew swayed onto the dance floor because the top of the *maruni's* head barely reached the young officer's

17

chest.

The drummers beat their *madals* faster and faster as Andrew whirled to the music of *Naini Tal*: of the girl in the hill station with eyes blackened by *kajale* and hair shiny with oil, who would give the gallant sahib a night to remember.

Andrew's present night seemed to explode into brilliant pieces. Faces flashed before him, distant one moment, close up the next, blurred. Wasn't this the colonel? Tottering a bit on his feet. He was pumping Andrew's hand.

'Well done! It was worth it just to see the look on Roger's face.'

I wonder what he means? Andrew thought. Who the hell is Roger?

There were other faces and more rum, then everything became jumbled and the next thing he knew he was being helped back to his quarters by three members of his winning team. He wondered why Tekbir wasn't there, and he was disappointed that the havildar was so unfriendly.

'Where is Tekbir?' he demanded.

'Flat on his back,' said Jitbahadur, giggling because he had drunk quite a few *rakshis* himself. 'He had even more than you, Sahib.'

'Oh, I see,' said Andrew through an intoxicated haze as he staggered onto the verandah and into his bedroom. He vaguely remembered being undressed. Then he was lying on the *charpoy*, and the room was spinning and he thought he was going to be ill, but sleep was kind to him.

When he awoke the following morning he felt dreadful, as, in fact, did practically everyone in the battalion. But Jitbahadur and Tekbir were already dressed, and, with splitting headaches, making their way to an important meeting with the subedar-major.

Ganje Thapa showed no sign of being any the worse on the morning after the night before. He was immaculately turned out and looked in the best of health as he invited them to sit down, although, in reality, his head was thumping like one of last night's *madals*.

'That was some party,' he said. 'The best I remember for a long time – and a good send off for our departure to the front. And, of course, to acknowledge the magnificent win.

18

How is Miller Sahib?'

'Sleeping it off, I should think,' said Tekbir.

Jitbahadur glared at him. But Ganje smiled briefly. He knew that Tekbir, for all his apparent truculence, was a loyal member of the battalion, and a good man to have with you in a tight situation.

'It is about Miller Sahib that we have come to see you,' Jitbahadur said. 'He has proved to be such a good basketball player that it would be disastrous to lose him. And the danger will certainly be there when we move into Burma. How could any Japanese sniper fail to pick him out as a prime target?'

Ganje agreed that it was a serious matter, and Jitbahadur suggested, 'Perhaps the Sahib could be transferred to the office – say as quartermaster's assistant?'

'No!' The subedar-major was quite emphatic. 'You cannot take away the birthright of so promising an officer. He already has a good knowledge of our language. And he has discovered that vital art of leadership. He will bring glory to himself and the battalion. I feel it very strongly.'

'But as such an obvious target he might not live long enough to win glory.'

'Then he must be protected. But how?' The subedar-major answered his own query. 'He must have a special security squad responsible for his safety, as much as is possible, of course. And what better choice, I say, than his own basketball championship team – ay?'

The subedar-major looked quite pleased with his splendid idea. 'The position of subedar in C Company is vacant at the moment,' he continued. 'You, Jitbahadur, will transfer to that position. Tekbir is already in C Company, so that presents no problem. Manbahadur and Ranjit are in D Company so we will arrange their transfer as well. And I will hold you all responsible for taking every step to watch over Miller Sahib, and in the interest of the battalion that means to the utmost sacrifice.'

He looked closely at them, but there was no sign of fear on either man's face, and he would have been surprised if there had been.

Jitbahadur and Tekbir left the subedar-major's quarters, no doubts in their minds that the transfers would go through. The adjutant might be a bit peeved, the colonel might have something to say in the adjutant's support, but when it came to the crunch the subedar-major was the strong man of the battalion and no colonel or adjutant would go against him lightly, especially in a matter which was obviously of such importance to the battalion. So Jitbahadur became a subedar in C Company and was joined by Manbahadur and Ranjit.

A few days later the 4/15th Gurkha Rifles boarded a train travelling north-eastwards to the Burma front. For the next few weeks the battalion marked time in Assam, carrying out military exercises, spending seemingly endless hours in transit camps, hearing stories of great battles and events from other soldiers on the way out, but still not involved in the action itself. Then there was a sudden bustle of activity and excitement as the colonel returned from a brigade meeting and called in all the company commanders.

Eventually Carter returned to C Company and gathered Andrew and the Gurkha officers about him. He told them how the Japs, after their defeat in Imphal, had retreated across the Chindwin, and the 14th Army had followed up and established bridgeheads. Now General Slim's plan was to smash the regrouping Japanese army on the plains of Shwebo, and part of his plan was a tie-up with 36th Division in the Indaw-Wuntho area, some fifty miles north of Shwebo.

In the first instance, the Burmese towns of Pinlebu and Pinbon had to be seized. These lay between the Chindwin and the Irrawaddy, and any force attacking them would have to negotiate the great escarpment of Zibyu Taungan which stretched north to south in a barrier of some 200 miles and rising to more than 2,000 feet. Speed was essential, but it would be some days before artillery and transport could be assembled east of the Chindwin. The brigade bound for Pinlebu would have to go ahead without support, so if the passes were strongly held by the enemy there would be considerable delay in the tortuous country of deep ravines and hill-clinging tracks. Air support would be of little use against a well-concealed position on a steep, thickly jungled ridge.

The force would have to operate like a Chindit Long-

Range Penetration Group, and as the 4/15th had trained for such a role, it was attached to the Pinlebu force as a pathfinder. Within a few hours the battalion was on its way in transport to Palel. From there it marched through the jungle down to the Chindwin, crossing the river in a fleet of boats and power-operated rafts.

Although Andrew's body was taut with a mixture of fear and excitement as the battalion moved towards the foothills, he could still admire the beauty of the jungle. Tall trees rose up to the umbrella of green foliage with patches of blue sky, and sunlight breaking through so that the creepers looked like lattice work, and the hillside curved down to a *chaung* where small pools reflected the afternoon sun. The sudden barking of a pack of monkeys echoed through the hills and into the vaults of the jungle. In the undergrowth there was a rustle followed by the sharp, drawn out wail of a hidden bird sounding like an engine whistle.

Then the first bivouac in Burma, awakening to a forest, cold and damp. In the dawn the teak trees were like gigantic columns supporting a roof of dark brown leaves. The haze of smoke from the cooking fires mingled with shafts of sunlight and there was a faint buzz of voices. Gurkhas in the distance, wearing their warm jerseys and cap comforters, looked like little statues of gnomes in an overgrown garden.

Following an early start that morning, a short march brought the column to the foot of the towering escarpment, unfriendly and covered in a pelt of foliage which could hide deep ravines, overgrown paths or Japs. The track followed the banks of a *chaung* – an orifice of the escarpment, opening a way through the rugged foothills rising on either side. The *chaung* was ominously silent, with sandbanks which looked in the distance like huge whales basking in the wintery sun.

The battalion pushed on as fast as the conditions allowed, taking a chance of being ambushed. After a while they left the *chaung* and climbed in single file higher into the escarpment, winding and weaving through an ever-changing pattern of vegetation. Dense thickets of bamboo and thorn-covered undergrowth tore at the skin like angry cats until it was criss-crossed with scratches that filled rapidly with blood. The vanguard forced its way through dark, depressing confines of undergrowth and snake-like creepers before coming suddenly into open forest with sunny glades and tall trees and ground carpeted with leaves that crackled under the feet. And then abruptly the trail would drop like a roller-coaster to some deep ravine, before rising on the other side and across a flat, comfortable piece of ground.

The pattern continued hour after hour until at last D Company – which was in the lead – was almost in sight of the pass into Pinlebu. Lieutenant-Colonel Talbot came up to confer with the company commander. 'We'll have a little recce, I think,' he said.

With a section ahead, he and the company commander followed the leaf-strewn track for about fifty yards until it widened appreciably and passed through a cut in the hills. To one side was a low hill, on the other was a steep rise to the top of a high hill which commanded the pass, and from where a machine-gun suddenly opened fire. More heavy firing followed, leaving two Gurkhas dead and a third wounded in the leg. The remainder of the section retreated quickly, carrying the wounded man, to rejoin the colonel round a bend in the track.

The sudden burst of fire had alerted the whole column. There was hardly any room for deployment, so the soldiers just waited with arms at the ready. After a while came the news that D Company was going to attack the hill where a strong Japanese rearguard had dug in.

Out of sight of the hill, the rest of the battalion waited until the crump of mortars announced the beginning of D Company's attack. Automatic and rifle fire followed and seemed to go on for hours, mingling with shouts and screams, while the forest trembled and the hills reverberated. Then the shooting and the shouting died away, apart from an occasional rifle shot.

Presently the colonel appeared, walking slowly towards C Company. He told Jackie Carter that D Company Commander had been seriously wounded and half of his men were casualties. 'I'm afraid it's rather a tough nut. The Japs have dug in really well, and they have a solid bunker on the top which is only approachable up a narrow track. D Company reached about half-way, but the fire was too fierce and casualties too high. A gallant effort.'

He paused for a moment, conscious that the order he had to give would lead to more casualties, but he knew he had no choice. 'I want you to go in now, Jackie. The rest of brigade will be coming up and time is short. Best of luck.'

Carter said to Andrew, 'Let's go up ahead and have a look.'

They moved forward with Jitbahadur and a section, past Battalion HQ and reached the position at the base of the hill held by the survivors of D Company. Carter looked up at the formidable razor-backed approach and, at that moment, a rifle bullet from somewhere in the wall of green jungle hit him in the head. Andrew was rooted to the spot by shock, not attempting to take cover until Jitbahadur shouted frantically, 'Get down, Sahib!'

Jitbahadur felt a great knot of fear in his stomach. Andrew was now in command of C Company, and what chance would he have of survival, knowing that the hill had to be taken? For a moment Jitbahadur was tempted to advise him to inform the colonel so that a senior officer could be sent forward to assume command. But he stopped himself in time. The basketball team might still have their giant centre, but how much of a man would he be?

'Sahib, you are in command now,' Jitbahadur said. And though he was sad at Carter's death, he felt proud to place his trust in *The Lamo Sahib*.

Andrew looked up at the hilltop from behind suitable cover. He was surprised to find that he was no longer afraid. Coming forward with poor Jackie he was sure that everyone would see him trembling, but now he felt quite calm. And in that moment he knew what had to be done.

When his platoon commanders and the sole surviving jemadar from D Company had joined him, Andrew said, 'Imagine the hill to be a basketball pitch, with the bunker as the opponent's goal. The object is to get close enough to throw in a grenade or two through the slits. And this is how we will do it. You remember the last move, the fast break with which we won the cup? That is what we will do here.'

He paused for a moment and the Gurkhas waited in awe.

'One group will go up the middle, another group to the left and a third to the right. I think that where the hill curves at the sides there will be room and cover for sure-footed men like yourselves to run in. Meanwhile, covering fire will be given by D Company, and from a C Company detachment. I noticed a ravine further back, leading up to the hill on our right. The C Company detachment will give covering fire from there.

'When the first three groups reach as far as they can go they will take up fire positions. Then Jitbahadur Sahib and a section will cut across from the right, between the centre and the left, and I will move up the right and throw in the grenades.'

Jitbahadur restrained himself with difficulty from suggesting that someone else should throw the grenades. *The Lamo Sahib* would not listen and in any case, even the subedar-major would agree that he really was the best person for that part of the attack.

Havildar Tekbir spoke up. 'I shall take the middle line.'

He added quickly: 'It was my position in the championship final,' and stared belligerently at Andrew, but the young officer made no objection.

The platoon commanders brought their men forward quickly, while a detachment climbed up the ravine and into the jungle-topped hill which afforded a line of fire to cover the attack. When all was ready, Andrew blew his whistle. The hill exploded with sound and flame as the covering fire opened up.

'*Ayo Gurkhali!*' screamed Tekbir as he sprang out into the open and ran up the razor-edged track, followed by his group. The flank groups also moved out taking the slippery, curving hillside with all the agility of their race. In spite of the covering fire, the Japanese machine-guns raked the track. Where the bodies of D Company dead still lay, now C Company men fell to join them.

Tekbir, unscathed in spite of the bullets which were all about him like angry bees, reached a rocky outcrop and threw himself behind it. He was joined by the survivors of his group, who kept their heads down as pieces of rock broke into splinters under small arms fire. The two flank groups had also gone to ground, but were in a better position, having suffered fewer casualties, and were able to bring more fire to bear on

24

the bunker.

'Now!' shouted Andrew, and Subedar Jitbahadur raced across with his detachment. The Jap machine-guns switched to the new target, while Andrew, carrying a haversack of grenades, set off with giant strides round the curve of the hill and up as the covering fire intensified and every available Gurkha weapon concentrated on the Japanese positions.

Andrew felt that his eardrums would burst as the hills hurled the roar of the battle backwards and forwards. And then he had reached the right flank position. Without hesitation he passed through that group and up the last few feet of almost sheer hillside. He was within a few strides of his target when out of the jungle which fringed the right of the bunker came three Japs. Andrew froze. He had no weapons, having concentrated on the grenades.

But the first blast of fire came from over his shoulder as tommy-gun bullets ripped open one of the Japs, smashed the second's face to pulp and the last bullet in the magazine hit the third through the heart almost in the same instant as the man fired.

Andrew felt that last burst from the dying Jap fan his face, and heard a groan behind him. He turned. Tekbir lay on the ground. 'Go on Sahib!' the havildar called out. 'Score the goal!'

Andrew swung back to face the bunker, took a few steps, grenade in hand. Pulling out the pin, he rose in a great leap to hurl the grenade into the bunker. As he landed back on his feet and reached for a second grenade there was a flash of light behind the machine-gun slit, then an explosion, followed by an even greater detonation. Andrew was knocked off his feet and rolled down the hill.

There must have been some high explosives in the bunker to cause the huge blast which tore its roof apart, and hurled the heavy timbers crashing into the deep ravine below. In the crumpled, blackened ruin someone was screaming. From the Gurkhas came a shout of triumph as they raced up the hill, winkling out any of enemy who had escaped death.

Andrew's fall came to a halt when he collided with Ranjit and Manbahadur who helped him up, anxious to know if he had suffered any hurt. Even Jitbahadur had come running, breathless, thankful that Andrew was still unharmed.

'Where is Tekbir?' Andrew asked anxiously.

'Here he is, Sahib.'

Two medical orderlies were about to lift Tekbir onto a stretcher. His brown face was tinged with yellow, his eyes closed, and a great patch of blood had spread across his chest. But he opened his eyes as Andrew approached.

'That was the best pass I ever threw,' Tekbir said. Then, as the stretcher-bearers lifted him up. 'And you were not so bad yourself, *Lamo Sahib.*'

Johnny Gurkha Frenchman

When the German-commandeered train, taking forced labour into France, was derailed on the night after D-Day, the sudden, violent lurch brought Dulbir Rana instantly awake. As the wagon jumped the rails he clung desperately to the ridged sides to stop being propelled into the melée of flailing arms and legs. There were screams of agony and shouts of fear, and heads cracked against metal as the ball of tangled men was hurled backwards and forwards until with a final, shuddering crash the wagon came to rest on its side.

Dulbir's head was buzzing and there was a taste of blood in his mouth from a cut lip. Around him men were shouting, cursing, crying, but his attention was drawn to a gap about four feet above his head where the violence of the derailment had forced open the sliding doors.

He was doubtful of reaching it. But a Frenchman he had once befriended bent down so that Dulbir could climb onto his back and grasp the edge of the gap. With an effort the Gurkha then pulled himself up and used his legs against the sides to force his body through the opening until he lay flat along the top of the wagon.

Whistles, shouts and cries were coming from all along the train. The escaping steam from the shattered engine hissed like a giant serpent, and in the distance there was the crackle of Sten and Schmeisser.

Dulbir looked down into the wagon again to help the Frenchman up, but the man shook his head. Only then did Dulbir realize that his friend had hurt his arm and could not pull himself up. 'Go,' the man shouted, waving his good hand. Sadly, Dulbir climbed down from the wagon and within a few strides was hidden in some bushes beyond the track. Nobody else seemed to be taking advantage of the open door, and none of the German guards had come to check. Dulbir reckoned that they were too involved with the saboteurs or possibly had even been injured in the crash. Grenades crunched in the distance, the night sky flared red.

The young Gurkha checked his position. Beyond the railway the ground appeared to rise quite steeply to a wooded crown. In between there was not much cover, but in the darkness only a sharp movement would give him away. He made one last check to make certain no guard had returned to the wagon, then he climbed the slope, taking advantage of the night and what cover there was, all the noise around the derailed train still loud behind him. Every shout sent a tremor through his body in case he had been seen, but at last he reached the top and rolled over into the shelter of the forest.

The trees grew close together and in the darkness the tangle of undergrowth seemed like a wire fence as he fought his way through into the heart of the wood. The going became easier and he emerged suddenly onto a path running north and south. He crawled back into the undergrowth to work out his next move.

This was Dulbir's second escape. Now he remembered the depressing moment when he had been recaptured, and he was determined not to be taken again. He had first been taken prisoner at Tobruk in 1942, when Rommel's Afrika Korps was sweeping aside the British Eighth Army.

Dulbir, who was then in his early twenties, was a *naik*, a corporal, in the Commando Platoon of the 3/15th Gurkha Rifles. Out on patrol, the platoon had been cut off, but managed to reach Tobruk where it was placed under the command of the 2/7th Gurkha Rifles, one of the formations defending the thirty-five mile perimeter. On 20 June, hundreds of Stukas tore out of the desert sky, enemy artillery pounded the British positions, and the tanks of 21st Panzer Division rumbled menacingly over the horizon. By the evening the Germans had broken into the centre of Tobruk leaving the 2/7th and the 2nd Camerons still in defence on either side.

Dulbir remembered that long, hot day, choked by thick columns of smoke from burning vehicles, stores and petrol. The Gurkhas had to resist with little more than their courage and skill – there was no reserve ammunition nor any anti-tank guns. They held out through the night, but at 13.00 hrs on the 21st, with their ammunition nearly exhausted and the growing menace of enemy tanks, the Gurkhas' colonel surrendered.

For Dulbir it was a dreadful moment. But the words of courage and advice from his platoon commander, young Murray Sahib, helped him as he was taken off into captivity with the other Gurkhas who were separated from the British officers. Some of the men were sent to POW camps in Italy, Dulbir was among those transported to Germany.

It was in 1943 that Dulbir at last managed to escape, but a Gurkha in Nazi Germany was as obvious as a polar bear in a tropical jungle, and although he tried to avoid populated areas, hunger forced him to blunder into captivity again.

He fell into the hands of the Gestapo, and was still haunted by the memory of that terrifying time in their custody. And when the Gestapo no longer found him entertaining, they played a final devilish trick by sending him to a labour camp although well aware of his true identity. It said much for Dulbir's character that he was able to withstand the following months, deprived of fellow Gurkha prisoners, having to live and work in appalling conditions and unable to speak the many languages of his fellow captives. But he kept himself in good shape and he had remained alert. He had moved quickly to take advantage of the open door.

In the distance he could still hear muffled shouts, but the skirmish seemed to have ended. He left the shelter of the undergrowth, and returning to the path decided he would head north where there might be a chance of meeting friends.

The path was firm beneath Dulbir's feet as he loped along in the darkness, making good speed to put as much distance between him and the train as possible, but still alert for any sudden confrontation. The faintest of sounds somewhere ahead brought him to a halt. He stood quite still and listened carefully. There it was again, the metallic click of a weapon, a faint murmur of voices, but going away from him. He followed carefully, soon reaching a junction in the track where another path had wound its way up the hill. The group ahead must be French, Dulbir thought, perhaps some of the saboteurs involved in the fight. If they were, then they would surely be friendly. But he sensed the need for caution.

As he continued along the ridge the dawn came up quickly, the forest took shape, and he caught sight of the group in front. There were three men and they did not seem to expect trouble, for they paid no attention to their rear and wandered casually along the path through the forest. A moment later they turned off the ridge, taking another path which twisted through woods into a steep-sided valley. A slight mist, dispersing quickly, revealed green fields and vineyards, and a farmhouse among apple and cherry trees. The three Frenchmen followed a cart-track skirting the fields and went into the farmhouse. The barking of a dog sounded clearly for a moment across the valley to where Dulbir crouched behind cover.

In the farmhouse a middle-aged man, with a definite military bearing in no way concealed by countrified clothes, and with a face drawn from lack of sleep, welcomed the arrivals. 'But where is François?' he asked.

The men looked at each other, reluctant to speak.

'What is it? *Mon Dieu!* Maurice?'

A short, stocky man in his twenties, with unruly black hair, murmured, 'Dead, Patron.'

The patron slumped onto a chair with a gasp of anguish.

'We derailed the train as planned. It was a good job,' said Maurice gently. 'François placed the charges well, and the engine and most of the wagons jumped the rails. But as we were leaving we bumped into a Boche patrol. François was killed at once, the rest of us managed to escape – but after giving a hot reply.'

'Are you sure he was dead?'

'A burst of Schmeisser at point-blank range.'

'You had to leave the body, no doubt, but was nothing on him? No incriminating papers to show he was a British officer?'

'You know François, Patron. Would he have gone into action with anything like that on his person? No, no, Patron,

30

he will have been clean. The Boche will put him down as another Maquisard.'

The patron had organised the Maquis in the area, planning in particular for the Allied invasion when they could help to sabotage the German occupation forces. The Maquis had originated in the late summer of 1942 when the Germans pressured Laval to introduce the *Service du Travail Obligatoire,* to obtain forced labour for Germany from all Frenchmen of military age.

Many young Frenchmen had fled into the hills to escape the horror of the labour camps and had formed Maquis groups – in effect guerilla bands varying considerably in size. At first they were not very effective, being more concerned in fighting off the winter and coping with rough conditions than the Germans. To begin with they received little attention from the Germans who did not see them as any significant security risk. But as D-Day approached, the value of the Maquis became apparent to the Allies' planners, and arrangements were made for military equipment to be flown in and for British officers to train the men.

The patron wearily rubbed a hand over his face. François, the code-name for the British officer parachuted into France some weeks earlier, had been a demolition expert. With him gone, the programme of sabotage in the wake of the Normandy invasion would be drastically curtailed. And he had received information that the Boche would be sending a petrol train within the next few days. How were the Maquis going to blow it up now?

Jean, a burly young man who had been standing at the kitchen window called out. 'Patron, someone is coming. One man. He looks strange.'

'Strange?' The patron stood up to join Jean at the window. 'Hm. Could be Chinese.'

M'sieur Dubois, the farmer, said, 'It is nobody that I know.'

'Claude,' The patron nodded at the third Maquisard who moved out of the kitchen door.

Dulbir sensed the movement and saw the Sten. He raised his hands in the air and called out *'Ami! Ami!'*

Claude signalled with his gun for Dulbir to advance, which he did, but still keeping his hands up in case the Frenchman had a nervous trigger finger. From the window the patron watched Dulbir's approach and guessed he was a soldier, or had been. The well-worn boots, the battle-dress trousers, patched and baggy, the torn, khaki jersey, were hardly smart, but the patron liked the man's bearing. 'Let him in,' he told Claude.

When Dulbir entered the kitchen he almost felt like weeping, for there was warmth, the smell of good food, the homely atmosphere that he had missed for many years. But he also realized that there was hostility in the eyes of the Frenchmen. In the life they led anything unusual was to be treated with suspicion. And he guessed he must seem unusual.

The patron asked him who he was. This must be the commander, Dulbir thought, wishing that he had an ear for languages. He had a few words of German, French, Polish, Dutch, but only a few. He shook his head to indicate that he did not speak French, but guessed the question when the patron pointed at him. 'Gurkha,' he said. The patron looked blank. 'Gurkha,' Dulbir repeated. 'Johnny Gurkha,' he added in case that nickname was familiar in France.

'Perhaps he is Annamese from Cochin,' Maurice suggested – these were the days before the name was changed to Vietnamese.

'Most unlikely,' the patron disagreed. 'He does not speak French.'

In desperation, Dulbir held his hands together to indicate that he had been a prisoner of the Germans, and imitated a train and an explosion. Then forced his hands apart to show he had got free.

This time the patron nodded his head in understanding. 'He must have been in a labour gang. Did we know what the train was carrying?'

'No, Patron,' Maurice answered. 'The wagons were all closed. They must have been herded in like cattle.'

'Tobruk,' Dulbir said, holding his hands together again, 'Tobruk.'

The patron instantly looked more interested.

'Rommel,' Dulbir added.

Just then Madame Dubois came in. 'Now, now. What is this? No one eating? You must be starved.' She fussed around laying rolls of bread, large pats of butter, a ham, a jug of milk on the oil-cloth covered kitchen table. When she noticed Dulbir she asked who he was.

'We do not know,' her husband replied. 'Johnny, I think he is called. Escaped from the labour gang.'

'Chinese,' she suggested.

'No! Gurkha!' Dulbir exclaimed. Feeling quite desperate now. 'Gurkha!'

Madame Dubois looked keenly at him for a moment, then she raised her hands. 'Ah! Of course! I remember during the last war I was a girl at Marseilles and troops from India landed there in 1914 on the way to the front line. Crowds turned up to welcome them to our country. And the little Gurkhas, how they made us laugh . . . they had been given warm underclothes for the first time in their lives, and they were wearing them over their outer garments as they marched through the streets.'

Claude sneered. 'They do not sound like fighting men.'

'Oh but they were. We heard of how hard and gallantly they fought at Neuve Chapelle and many other places. We saw many wounded coming through later.'

'What are we going to do with him now, Patron?' Maurice asked.

'Let us wait for Pierre to contact us with his report on the derailment. Meanwhile, food – the poor fellow looks quite faint with hunger.'

Indeed, after the pig's swill he had been living on it was a great feast for Dulbir. Madame Dubois was delighted as she hustled about, and made certain that he did not lack for quantity, and in the end the Gurkha signalled his surrender as he sat back feeling bloated for the first time for months.

He also felt relieved that this motherly Frenchwoman somehow or the other knew about the Gurkhas. He wished he understood how it was that she did – it was something to do with World War I he guessed. If he could have spoken the language he would have told her how his grandfather had given his life for France at that Battle of Neuve Chapelle.

Shortly after the meal, Pierre arrived on his bicycle and reported that the line was blocked but the Germans were expected to clear it quickly. there was no search out for Johnny Gurkha, and it seemed unlikely that he would be

33

missed from the mixed bunch in the labour force.

'What about François?' the patron asked.

'The Boche are satisfied that he is French. Arrangements are being made for his funeral in the village. The mayor will make certain he receives a hero's farewell.'

'Good,' said the patron. 'And now I think we must be away to the Maquis. I shall stay there for a night or two.'

'What about Johnny?' Maurice asked.

'He will come with us.'

Madame Dubois said, 'He could do with a change of clothes.'

'All right, we will leave in half an hour.'

Madame Dubois led Dulbir out of the kitchen and up the stairs to a room at the top of the farmhouse. 'It was my son's,' she said.

Dulbir could tell from the pain in her voice that she had lost someone dear to her. She rummaged in a trunk and came up with corduroy trousers, a shirt, a leather jacket and a pair of canvas shoes with rope soles. 'You were of a size,' she said. 'He was not at all like his father or me.' The large homely woman smiled wistfully, then left the room.

A short time later, when Dulbir returned to the kitchen, Madame Dubois pressed a hand to her ample bosom.

'Yes, I thought he was your size.' And the patron nodded his head in approval at Dulbir's new appearance. Dulbir was slightly taller than the average Gurkha, with the light brown colour of a Rana.

'You'll do well,' the patron said. '*Bon. Bon!*'

Dulbir snapped to attention without thinking. 'Huzoor.'

The patron's eyebrows lifted slightly. Yes, this one was definitely a military man, and one who could be useful, especially if he had fought the Germans in the desert.

'*Au revoir Madame. M'sieur.* It was kind of you to give Johnny those clothes and all of us such a handsome breakfast.'

Pierre mounted his bicycle and returned to the village, the others left the farmhouse, through the apple orchard and along a path. Madame Dubois watched until they had disappeared from sight in the thick woods which covered the far hill.

Dulbir was not as fit as he used to be, but the pull of the climb on his muscles was as potent as a tot of rum. He felt quite heady and exhilarated, a hillman again, in his imagination climbing the Himalayan tracks, and when they entered a pine forest the illusion was enhanced.

They followed a path through fairly wild country until at last Maurice whistled and was answered. Leaving the path, and beyond some bushes and clusters of trees, they came out into a clearing and the Maquis camp.

The two parties greeted each other. There were eight men in the camp. Dulbir noticed – young men, looking at him suspiciously, Stens in hand. There was a chatter of conversation which Dulbir did not understand. He stood slightly apart, appraising the camp layout of two log cabins and a separate enclosure with a table and benches where the Maquis had their meals.

And then he saw the Bren gun. It was his favourite weapon, and he could not bear to see it lying there, in very poor condition, muddy, grimy, tottering on its bipod. Nearby a cluster of magazines were stacked anyhow on the ground.

He moved towards the Bren and sat on his haunches beside the beautiful, gas operated light machine-gun, a thorough-bred, which gave hardly any trouble when treated with proper respect. It looked like one of the new Mks – probably dropped by parachute recently, and just discarded, he guessed, because it would no longer fire – and no one knew how to rectify any fault or strip it down.

Dulbir ran his hands over the gun with an affection which made itself manifest to the Maquisards who had stopped talking and were watching him in anticipation. He made a sign to Maurice, and some parachute cloth was brought and laid down by the gun, together with flannelette, oil and a pull-through.

The Gurkha took off his leather jacket and placed it carefully to one side. Then his hands moved expertly lacking none of the skill developed under the tough tuition of the training jemadar at his regimental centre in India. He had practised for hours until he could strip the gun and put it together again blindfolded. Now the Maquisards could not prevent their cries of astonishment and delight as Dulbir stripped the gun with lightning speed. With the pieces spread on the parachute cloth, he began to clean the gun, bit by bit. None of the parts seemed damaged, and by the time he had put the Bren together again it gleamed.

Then he picked up a magazine, removed the thirty .303 bullets, flexed the spring, made a face. Still, it was not too bad, had not been maltreated long enough for permanent damage. Then he reloaded the magazine, with twenty-eight bullets so as not to strain the spring, indicating to the Frenchmen how it should be done to ensure that each round was fed in with the rim behind the one in front.

Maurice asked him, 'Do you want to test the gun?' making the appropriate signs. And at Dulbir's eager nod led the way out of the camp, around the back and down into a re-entrant. A square of parachute cloth was placed at the far end, held down by stones, and Dulbir lay down behind the gun, pulling the butt into his shoulder like returning to a lover after a long absence. With the gun on single shot he squeezed the trigger, but nothing happened. Leaning forward he slipped the barrel out of its socket, adjusted the gas block, replaced the barrel. This time the gun fired, the bullet left of centre, about an inner. He tried a few more single shots until he placed a shot in the centre. Then he switched to automatic and fired a couple of controlled bursts which made a neat group pattern.

The patron took Maurice to one side. 'We will be sending a broadcast to London tonight to ask for another British officer, but I do not think there is any chance he will arrive in time for the petrol train.' He nodded towards Dulbir, surrounded by the excited Maquis.

'Do you think he might also be a demolition expert?'

'He is certainly a soldier,' Maurice replied. 'And a good one, well-trained in weaponry. Demolition is usually more specialized – even in his army, I should think.'

'We can ask him, but can we trust him?'

Maurice suggested that they could get a demolition man from another Maquis outside their area. The patron did not look very pleased. The destruction of the petrol train would give him great satisfaction and a reputation, and he did not want to pass this on a plate to some outsider, even in the war's interest, if he could possibly prevent it.

'He is no spy, Patron. No Boche agent, if I am sure of anything it is that. And the way Madame Dubois accepted him – I do not think she could be fooled.'

So in the morning the patron and Maurice took Dulbir further up the hill to another shelter where the Maquisard pulled aside a tarpaulin to reveal a store of demolitions.

'Do you know anything about these, Johnny?'

Dulbir had already given Maurice an answer by his quick approach to the cache and his keen examination of its contents. There were several pounds of plastic explosive in 8oz cartridges in grease paper, a small quantity of Nobels 808, boxes of detonators, primers, Bickford's safety fuse, fire matches, pull switches, time pencils, cordtex detonating fuse, incendiaries. The Gurkha looked up, grinning at the Frenchman, and pointed at his chest. 'Commando Platoon,' he said. 'Commando Platoon!'

'He must have been in some commando unit,' Maurice said.

'We have a big job to do, Johnny.' The patron pointed towards the distance in the direction of the railway, giving an imitation of an explosion.

Dulbir nodded his head vigorously. To get back at the Germans was all he sought. 'When is the job, Patron?' he asked, pointing to his wrist to indicate time.

The patron smiled at Dulbir's use of 'Patron'. Then shrugged his shoulders to indicate that he did not know at this stage.

Maurice covered up the explosives and the three men then returned to the main camp where they found Pierre waiting.

'There is more news about the petrol train. Its arrival has been advanced to tonight.'

'*Mon Dieu!*' The patron threw up his arms in anguish.

Maurice said, 'But the line is blocked.'

'No. A large rail gang and crane opened the line by early this morning. The train is due to go through around 2.15 tomorrow morning.'

'That could mean several hours later,' the patron said in exasperation.

'Not this one.' Pierre was confident. 'The Boche want it forward urgently. And it will have a strong escort.'

'We could cut the line,' Maurice suggested. 'That would delay its arrival. Give us another day.'

'Maybe,' Pierre agreed, 'but it will make the Boche more

alert when they do come through. By changing the schedule so drastically they believe they will have the element of surprise. What is more they are only sending through eight of the petrol tank wagons.'

'Then it must be tonight,' the patron said wearily. 'Call the men around and we will discuss it.' The Maquisards were excited at the prospect, but when Dulbir realized that it was to be that night he was disturbed. 'Reconnaissance first,' he said.

The patron shook his head. '*Non. Non.* No time.'

Dulbir looked stubborn. 'Must go first,' he insisted. '*L'essence*' – he had picked up the word for petrol – 'difficult.' He had to explain to the Frenchmen that simply derailing the train was no guarantee that the petrol would ignite. Ideally it needed a cutting charge to release the petrol from the tank into the air, and an incendiary placed to catch the flowing liquid a few seconds later, and not the first gush. He picked up a fallen twig and drew a line in the dust. 'Train,' he said. He then pointed the stick at the front and back. 'Boche.'

'*Oui. Oui,*' Pierre confirmed. '*L'Boche escort.*'

The Gurkha pointed to the middle. '*L'essence.*'

Pierre nodded. 'Eight wagon *citernes.*'

'First the train should be derailed,' Dulbir said with appropriate signs, 'and attacks put in on both front and back escorts. If the crash has not set off the petrol, then I and another man run to the petrol tank wagons, place the explosion and incendiaries and retreat. Immediate explosion. Then the rest of the Maquis break off the action and return to camp.'

The Maquisards spoke among themselves in rapid French which Dulbir could not follow, but he attracted their full attention again with a sketch in the dust, indicating that the ideal spot would be a bend in the track passing through a cutting with good slopes on either side. His idea was to derail the engine on a straight section, isolating the rear escort and say a couple of tank wagons round the bend. And while he placed the charges – out of the line of fire – the Maquisards could keep the rear escort pinned down. In all likelihood the front escort's carriage would be derailed with the engine, and any of the enemy who survived the crash could easily be taken out of the action.

Claude, who was a local boy, said excitedly, 'I know just the place.'

'That will save time at least,' the patron said.

Maurice suggested, 'Why not use the Citroën at the Dubois farm?' And so it was agreed.

Soon afterwards, Dulbir with Maurice, Pierre and Claude returned to the farm. Maurice drove the big, black Citroën out of the garage, the others joined him in the car, and Madame Dubois waved as they drove along the track, through woods, out onto a country lane.

Maurice seemed to be able to drive only at top speed, and Dulbir wondered what would happen if they came across the Germans. They approached the outskirts of the village where Claude asked Maurice to stop. 'There is a path here through the woods. It will take us straight to the place I know.'

'Then you and Johnny go,' said Maurice. 'Pierre and I will continue to the village, and return to pick you up here in, say, two hours.'

As the car accelerated away, Claude led Dulbir off the road and onto a path through the woods which they followed for about half an hour until it came out on the railway.

'What do you think, Johnny? *Bon?*'

From the edge of the wood they looked down a steep slope to the track, and beyond it another rise to the hill on the far side. Approaching from the left, the track followed a fairly sharp bend, swinging left-handed through the cutting, straightening out gradually.

'*Bon,*' Dulbir agreed. They stepped out of the trees and ran down the cutting slope and across a ditch to the railway. Flatfooted rail, Dulbir thought, fastened to the sleeper by pins on the bottom flange, fairly simple to remove a piece of track. But he decided that he would rather use fog signals to detonate a charge.

They walked along the track to the bend. The wall of the cutting was dotted with bushes and ascended to the wooded hilltop, which seemed an ideal position for a group of the Maquis to overlook the rear escort and bring heavy fire to bear.

Retracing his steps, Dulbir calculated the point where he would place the rail cutting charge. From the hill above another group of the Maquis could account for any of the front escort who survived the derailment. Meanwhile, he and another man would move down the slope, place the charges and return to cover. The ditch, which was about five feet wide and the same in depth would need to be bridged, because he did not want to jump across weighed down with explosives. He had seen some suitable planks at the farm, and he made a mental note to pick one up that night.

'*Bon! Bon!*' Dulbir said to Claude. The Frenchman grinned appreciatively. He was only a youth of eighteen or nineteen, slim but wiry, and not much taller than Dulbir. He tapped the Gurkha's chest with a finger, then his own, and pointed to the railway.

'We two,' he said. 'You take me as your bodyguard when you go to blow up the train.' He swung his hands around like a Sten spitting out lead.

Dulbir grinned. '*Oui,*' he agreed.

They returned through the woods to the rendezvous with Maurice, waiting behind bushes from where they could watch the road. Almost at once there was the sound of an engine in the distance and both men tensed, expecting the black Citröen to come speeding into view, but it was a van running on charcoal and woodchips which spluttered past.

Ten minutes later they heard another car, and moved to the roadside when Maurice swept round the corner in the Citröen, bringing it to a screaming halt. They scrambled quickly into the back, and he was away, changing rapidly into top gear.

After parking the car in the garage at the farm, they returned to the Maquis camp. It was early afternoon, and the patron was relieved to see them. The others had eaten their midday meal, and Maurice and Pierre had been well fed in the village, so while Dulbir and Claude tackled the bread, butter and ham which Madame Dubois had pressed on them at the farm, and a bottle of wine with the compliments of the patron, they discussed *Operation Essence.*

Claude described the lay out, between mouthfuls, and the others discussed the tactics and evolved the plan. It was decided to approach the railway in two groups. Jean, who was appointed Bren gunner, and four men were to take an out-of-the-way route through the wooded hills; Maurice with Dulbir, Claude and three men to proceed via the farm where the patron would spend the night. Pierre left straightaway. He would keep a check on the train's timetable through his contact in case of any last minute changes.

After the meal, Dulbir climbed further up the hill with Claude to the explosives cache and prepared the charges for the night's work. He had decided to use the plastic, moulding the yellow, putty-like explosive into blocks with primers, and embedding magnets to hold the explosive to the target. He did not know how much time he would have, but he decided to make four charges. He also prepared flares to set the petrol alight and the explosives to derail the train. When he was ready, he packed the charges in the rucksack provided, keeping the firing systems separate.

Jean's group left first as they had the furthest to travel – Jean carrying the Bren proudly over a shoulder, the remainder armed with Stens. About an hour later the patron and Maurice ambled down to the farm, followed by Dulbir and the second group of Maquisards.

The long shadows of twilight lay across the valley. The distant river, winding through the willows, flashed an occasional heliograph of silver in the fading power of the sun, a message to Dulbir to remember home, his own valley in the Himalayas which was rougher hewn and more garish than the finer tones and pastel shades of the French valley. But a view of any distant valley from hillsides aroused the same sensation and that was what Dulbir felt: free! And beyond the valley was the railway where he would experience again the excitement of going into action; but armed this time, powerful and destructive, not helpless against those rat-faced Gestapo.

The Maquis came down from the hills to the farm as darkness finally filled the valley. The patron wished his men good luck as they continued across the valley and up the far wooded slopes, Claude leading the way along a path tunnelled through the forest, and one of the Maquisards carrying the plank to bridge the ditch.

'We are nearly there,' Claude said at last. The rest waited while he went forward, moving stealthily. When he returned he reported no sign of Jean.

'We'll go on to the railway,' Maurice said.

A few minutes walk brought them to the edge of the wood. Dulbir, his eyes accustomed to the darkness, looked down at the railway and beyond to the far hill. The night was quiet. And then he picked up a metallic click, and the sound of bodies pushing aside undergrowth, and signalled to the others to keep quiet. A few moments later there was a whistle. Claude replied. The dark shadows of Jean's group joined and mingled with the others.

'You had no difficulty?' Maurice asked softly.

'Not really,' Jean said. 'We thought we heard a Boche patrol some way back, but they were not moving in this direction.'

'All right. We have about three hours to wait for the train if it is on time – and that Pierre will tell us. Meanwhile we will spread out into firing positions.'

Dulbir guided Jean and four Maquisards to the position he had selected overlooking the bend in the track, while Claude led three more to the position covering the front of the train. They both then returned to the central position to join Maurice.

The night remained quiet except for the occasional cry of some predator unfamiliar to Dulbir. In the woods above his own home he would have recognised every call. He was thinking this when he picked up the sound of a train and sat up abruptly. Maurice placed a restraining hand on his shoulder. '*Non. Non.* Passenger train 1.15 *le civil.*' As Dulbir saw the train grow into shape out of the dark and rattle past, the engine hissing, it gave him an additional yardstick to the possible length of the petrol train and where to place the charges to cut the line.

A moment later Pierre arrived, breathless, and rather frightened. '*Mon Dieu!* I thought I would never find you. There seems to be a great deal of Boche activity tonight.'

'What about the train?' Maurice asked impatiently.

'It left on time,' Pierre said, still breathless. 'Should be here in an hour or so.'

'Well done, Pierre.' Maurice then explained the situation to Dulbir who wasted no time in picking up his rucksack and descending the slope with Claude who carried the plank to bridge the ditch.

The Gurkha had already prepared the railcutting charges. He had cut a length of detonator fuse five metres long, doubled, and with six inches left over at one end; and threaded on two primers from one end, one metre apart. Around each primer he had moulded the explosives. He also had fog signals to fire the charge.

Now he laid down the firing system beside the track, the fog signals towards the direction of the incoming train. Then he taped on the first charge, stretched the detonator fuse tight and taped on the second charge. He clipped the fog signals on to the rail, ensuring that the detonators were to the outside, and checked the detonator fuse connecting the charges to see that it was fully extended. At the top of each fog signal were three percussion caps and a quantity of quickmatch.

When he was satisfied that all was properly set up, he led Claude back into the woods to rejoin Maurice and Pierre, leaving the plank in position across the ditch. They all settled down to wait again, growing more nervous, more tense as the time approached, hearing all manner of strange sounds in the woods, expecting a German patrol to appear suddenly with Schmeissers blazing.

But at last came the sound they had been waiting for; and presently the train puffed around the bend, a blur lit up by sparks from the engine. It carried along the straight stretch; engine, converted carriage for the German escort, and seven petrol tank wagons. The eighth tank wagon and the rear escort's carriage were still on the bend when the heavy engine wheels crushed the fog signals detonating the charges and the explosion thundered between the hills, smoke and dust whitening the night like ghosts.

The engine dipped, left the track, roaring out its death-throes like some great animal hit by the hunter's bullets, taking the front escort's carriage and the first tank wagon with it. A coupling snapped and the rest of the train came to a grinding, tearing halt but remained upright.

The sound of the explosion was still in the air as the Maquisards on the right opened fire on the few survivors from the front escort who were trying to scramble out of their wrecked carriage. The Germans slithered in their own blood, and their cries mingled with the hiss of escaping steam and the chatter of the Stens.

The Maquis on the left also opened fire, but the rear escort reacted quickly. A Spandau hammered out into the night, rapping the wooded hill. Volleys of small-arms fire were discharged from the carriage windows. Jean brought his Bren into action, bullets penetrating the rear carriage, searching for the Spandau, finding it, pinning the gunner against the far wall with a riveting burst.

But the petrol was still intact, so Dulbir and Claude bounded down the slope and over the plank. Dulbir ran towards the third tank wagon from the front. Near at hand it seemed huge as he climbed up the inspection ladder attached to its cylindrical side and clamped on the first charge, the powerful magnets gripping like a tiger's claws hooked into the side of an elephant. He then taped the incendiary flare further down. Inserting the length of safety fuse already prepared into the detonator, he crimped it and thrust it into the hole in the primer.

The rear escort was still firing at the Maquis on the hill, but no bullets were coming in his direction so he decided to place all his charges before ignition.

Moving on, he clamped explosive charges only on the fourth and fifth tanks, then ran to the sixth, clambering up to clamp on the second charge and incendiary, and now he set the timed fuse alight. Next he retraced his steps to light the fuse on tank five, and was about to set off tank four when bullets fanned his face and ricocheted off the metal, whistling into the night.

Three Germans had crept in from the far side, climbing between the two tank wagons at the rear. Claude returned the fire and one of the Germans fell to the ground. Then Claude cried out, clasping his head, his Sten flung up in the air as he collapsed. Dulbir was weaponless, and he braced himself for the next burst of Schmeisser bullets to smash him against the side of the tank. But at that moment several pinpoints of light flashed along the hill above and the Germans were caught in a fusillade of Sten gun fire. One man dropped his weapon, slithered down the side of a tank, leaving a trail of blood. The remaining German collapsed to his knees as his legs were shattered. With great courage he tried to bring his Schmeisser into a firing position, but another burst of Sten riddled his chest. As he died he still managed to press the trigger, but the bullets passed harmlessly into the night.

The whole incident had taken only a few seconds, but time was running out, and Dulbir quickly lit the fuse of tank four's charge. Ignoring Claude who still lay on the ground, Dulbir ran to tank three and lit the charge and incendiary fuses. Jumping down, he ran back to Claude, and as he did so Maurice came up beside him. Claude groaned as they lifted him up. The first fuse must be nearly at ignition point, Dulbir thought, desperately.

But thankfully the young Frenchman was a lightweight, and they soon carried him to the ditch where the three of them took cover. Dulbir held Claude flat against the bottom of the ditch as the first charge exploded, and there was a great whoosh when the incendiary set off the petrol seconds later. Dulbir could feel the heat in the ditch as the second charge detonated and more petrol was ignited. The last two charges went off together; chunks of metal flew over the ditch like aeroplane engines soaring up the slope to slash a passage through the greenery of the woods before embedding in more solid tree trunks.

Red-hot debris from tank six spun along the side of the cutting and a large chunk shot through a window of the rear escort's carriage and into an open box of ammunition. There were cries of terror from the Germans who had held out against the Maquis, as the ammunition exploded and bullets criss-crossed the carriage. Suddenly the carriage caught fire and in a moment was a ball of flame. Figures like burning torches jumped screaming from the coach; ruthless Bren and Sten gun fire gave them a merciful end.

Dulbir was not sure if the attack was still on, or whether the crackle of bullets was ammunition exploding, so he decided to stay a bit longer in the safety of the ditch. Then Pierre poked his head over the edge of the ditch.

'Maurice! Johnny! Are you all right?'

They lifted Claude out and carried him up the hill. The young Frenchman was groaning as they set him down gently on the ground, his face covered in blood. In the light from the burning train, which flickered among the trees in a blood orange glow, one of the Maquisards, who had been a medical student before fleeing for his life from the Gestapo, wiped off the blood. 'Lucky man,' he diagnosed. 'Just a graze.' He took out a field dressing and bandaged Claude's head.

Claude sat up and groaned. '*Mon Dieu!* My head aches.'

'Can you walk?' Maurice asked.

They lifted Claude to his feet. 'A bit giddy,' he said. 'But I'll manage with some help.'

Maurice told Jean to return to the camp with his group and to take great care as the derailment was sure to have alerted Boche patrols. Then, with two men supporting Claude, and one to carry the plank in case it could be traced to the farm, Maurice led his group back along the path. There had been no other casualties.

After a short distance, Maurice turned off the path and climbed through open pine forest to join a woodcutter's path on the ridge which would take them to the farm from another direction. For a moment, through a gap in the forest, Dulbir could see the sky above the railway track glowing an angry red, with occasional tongues of yellow from the fire which still raged out of sight around the crumpled and blasted remains of the petrol tank train.

He felt Maurice's hand on his arm. 'Well done, Johnny.'

And this made up for the indignities and torture he had suffered at the hands of the Gestapo, the shame of the surrender at Tobruk. He was a Gurkha warrior again.

The Last Gamble

They deserved their reputation as the most compulsive gamblers the regiment had ever seen. Ganesh Gurung and Shere Thapa would take bets against each other, or anyone else, on anything from the normal run of cards to whether it would rain the next day.

But their most notorious gamble was made on the Western Front in 1914, and passed into the legends of the regiment.

A machine-gun team had rushed forward to give covering fire for an intended push by the battalion. Watching from the trenches, Ganesh noticed that the leading gunner had immediately been shot through the head.

As the number two took over, Ganesh said, 'I bet he will not last twenty seconds.'

'Done,' said Shere, losing almost as soon as he had accepted because the number two was wounded in the arm after firing a few bursts.

By this time the third gunner had taken over and an interested crowd of Gurkhas had gathered round the two gamblers. A roar of laughter arose as the unfortunate third gunner was hit.

But apart from being intrepid gamblers, Ganesh and Shere were keen soldiers. Shere at once shouted, 'The gun is unmanned!' He rushed forward with Ganesh at his heels, and got behind the machine-gun, bringing it immediately into action. He was a good shot, and his bullets found their target.

While changing the belt, Shere said, 'I bet I last more than five minutes.'

For once Ganesh hesitated, but the urge was too great and he accepted the wager.

About an hour later Shere was still behind the machine-gun, and the battalion had achieved its objective.

'I am glad I lost my bet,' Ganesh said. And then he noticed the blood spreading across Shere's chest. His friend had been hit much earlier but had carried on firing.

Although mortally wounded, Shere grinned. Then, with great difficulty, as there was blood in his mouth, he said softly, so softly that Ganesh could hardly hear him. 'I will give you a last chance. I bet you die before me.'

'You will not live long enough to pay my winnings,' Ganesh said jokingly. A second later the German sniper's bullet hit him in the head.

The American Sahib

'A Yank!' exclaimed Lieutenant-Colonel Butterworth, commanding officer of the 5/15th Gurkha Rifles.

'He could be a gentleman from the South,' suggested his adjutant.

'You know what I mean, John,' the colonel said sharply. 'An American. Joining our battalion.'

Not that the colonel was anti-American. But he believed that an American would be alien to the British environment of a Gurkha regiment – an environment evolved over many years because of that very special relationship between officers and men.

'But, sir,' the adjutant protested, 'two or three of the other Gurkha regiments already have Americans on their establishment.'

'I am well aware of that John. And I believe that one of them has been teaching his men to play craps.'

'He'd have met his match with our lot, sir. Especially C Company – they are the slickest bunch of gamblers I've ever come across.'

The colonel smiled. 'Perhaps we ought to post what's his name? – Paul Cooper – to C Company.'

At this time, Second-Lieutenant Paul Cooper was travelling from Bombay to Poona on *The Deccan Queen* to join the battalion. As the crack Indian express sped almost silently across the plain, Paul leaned back in his comfortable seat in the first-class compartment he had to himself. He was nervous, yet excited, because his wild ambition which had always seemed just a dream, was now to be fulfilled.

He had been at an English university, specializing in modern languages, when Britain declared war on Germany, and had almost volunteered to join up with his British friends, which had alarmed his father who was in England on business.

Paul had not seen a lot of his father until in his late teens. He had been a sickly child, and his mother had fussed over him, keeping him with her in New York where she had her friends and rich relatives, and had refused to accompany his father on his many business trips to Europe. At an early age, Paul reckoned that the marriage was foundering.

Paul's mother took him from one specialist to another, trying to find out why he was so sickly, so thin, so backward in his physical growth. His brain had been well ahead of his body, especially in learning languages, and he was soon fluent in French and German.

His mother had the money to spend on doctors, but it was all wasted until she finally found an honest, direct man who told her straight that she must let Paul lead a proper life, get out in the open. So he had spent a marvellous summer on a rich uncle's private beach, soaking in the sun and swimming. The change in him was quite miraculous within a year. He filled out, grew tall, and his muscles developed. And then his mother had been killed in an automobile accident.

Paul's father saved him from the grief which could have undone all the good work. After the funeral, they spent a holiday together in Europe where he got to know his father again, and because his father spent so much time in Europe, Paul was persuaded to complete his education at an English university.

At his father's request, Paul had agreed to delay enlisting until he had graduated the following year. Cooper senior hoped that by then the war would be over, or that his son might not be so keen to help other people fight their battles. But he was wrong on both counts.

Paul felt quite strongly that Britain's war with the Nazis was as much America's war, and that eventually the United States would have to enter the lists against Germany. Meanwhile, he could not stand aside and wait for that day. So it was with chagrin that he spent six months square-bashing on the parade ground and taking part in countless tactical exercises. But his keenness had not gone unnoticed, and when suitable officer material was sought he found himself on a troopship bound for India.

During Paul's service in the ranks, his nationality had not been a particular disadvantage, although everyone thought he had plenty of money – and, in fact, he was wealthy through his mother's estate, but he had the good sense not to try to buy friendship or recognition. He was accepted as a good soldier, but considered rather mad to take part in someone else's war. Yet the Irish and the Gurkhas had been doing it for years – and very well too.

His arrival at the Officers' Training School in Bangalore was an exciting experience. As a boy, *The Lives of a Bengal Lancer* had fired his imagination. He knew that the Indian Army could not be quite as glamorous as portrayed by Gary Cooper, but he was sure there was sufficient truth in the film to hold out an adventurous prospect.

He was lucky in his room-mate at OTS, who told him about the Gurkhas – and wondering how Gary Cooper had missed out in not making a film as an officer in the Gurkhas – Paul decided that here was what he had been looking for. Although he knew that even in wartime a posting to a Gurkha regiment would be difficult, he reckoned that he had gained sufficient experience of the British to overcome any initial problems.

At OTS, every cadet was allowed to name, in order of preference, three regiments he would like to join provided there was a vacancy. Naturally, Paul listed three Gurkha regiments, and to his delight was commissioned in the 15th Prince Albert's Own Gurkha Rifles, reporting for duty at the Regimental Centre in Quetta.

The three months at the Centre had been frustrating, and he was overjoyed when posted to the 5th Battalion down south in Poona. With the added bonus of a week's joining leave, he wasted no time in travelling to Bombay to accept an invitation from Christina, a girl he had met at Bangalore when she was there visiting friends. And it had been a marvellous few days in her Bombay flat overlooking the great sweep of the bay, the miles of golden sand extending to the green coolness of Malabar Hill.

The train had begun to climb into the Western Ghats, the high hill range which rises out of the plain in a steep barrier of rock and jungle, a challenge which has been met by inspired engineering. *The Deccan Queen* slipped suddenly into a long tunnel, and the lights came on in the compartment. Paul could see himself reflected in the window. He was just twenty, and a shade over six feet. His black hair was cut short, but in the regulation British officer style and not the crew cut which would have made him look American. Not that he was ashamed of his nationality but he just knew that appearance counted a lot when first being appraised. He was, after all, a good-looking young man, and his khaki uniform had been cut to achieve a regimental smartness. And his blue eyes had a glint of steel in them – at least that was what Christina had said as they lay beneath the ceiling fan, the whirring blades cooling their bodies after the heat of passion. That's why he was such a good lover, she had said.

The express came out of the tunnel with a sudden flash from darkness to sunlight. Sheer, black rock rose on both sides of the track, and rivulets of water ran down the rocky hillside wetting the ebony surface till it shone like a well-groomed racehorse. Like the horses at Bombay Racecourse, Paul thought, where he and Christina had attended a meeting still as colourful and exciting as in peace-time. But that was all part of a holiday now over.

When *The Deccan Queen* at last ran smoothly into Poona station, Paul felt his heart beating quickly. He tried to overcome his nerves by reminding himself that he did have an ace up his sleeve, although he was reluctant to use it to his immediate advantage. He was waiting for the right time when it would have the most impact, and something cautioned him to wait, that the moment had not yet come.

He stepped out into the corridor putting on his Gurkha hat – two bush-hats, one tucked into the other, the double brim stiffened all around, a black chin-strap polished to shine like a mirror, the crossed-kukris badge on a felt flash at the side.

Looking tentatively through the window at the crowded platform he saw two more Gurkha hats – one belonging to Captain Martin, C Company Commander; the other to a Gurkha orderly who quickly and efficiently organised coolies to carry Paul's luggage from the compartment and luggage-van to the 15 cwt truck waiting in the yard.

Martin was a short, stocky, bustling man in his late twenties and a regular commissioned officer. 'You're joining C Company as my company officer,' he said as they shook hands.

'Yes, sir,' Paul acknowledged, thinking that if his company commander could take the time to meet him in person, then it said a good deal for the battalion.

As they came out of the station, darkness fell abruptly, lights encircled the large station yard, and from an Indian café, music blared into the night.

Because it was *Diwali* everywhere little oil lamps flickered in honour of *Rama*. Firecrackers exploded and chattered like machine-guns, children shaped circles in the air with spluttering sparklers, and overhead rockets flared and streaked across the sky. Martin drove the truck out of the station approach into the stream of traffic.

'Our camp is at Kharakwasla,' he said. 'Attractive spot by the lake, and good training country.'

They left the confines of Poona Cantonment behind and continued along a tree-lined road. The headlights picked out a long column of bullock-carts wandering in the middle of the road. Martin overtook them without reducing speed, wheels churning the dust at the side of the road.

They drove in silence for the remainder of the journey which ended when the truck came round a corner and there was the wide expanse of Kharakwasla Lake, and on the hillsides the flickering oil-lamps of the Gurkha camp.

Early the next morning partridges were calling further up the hill as Paul walked the short distance from his hut to C Company lines. He was able to take in the full extent of the lake, which stretched into the distance, and the wooden huts of the camp neatly grouped on the hillside.

The Gurkhas ran about three miles every morning as individual companies. Paul, when told this the previous night by Martin, had immediately volunteered to take part.

'But you'll want to settle in,' the captain had said.

Paul had been persistent.

'OK,' said Martin. 'Then I'll have a morning off. I have some paper work to catch up with anyway.'

Paul was wearing just a pair of brief shorts and canvas shoes. Somewhat disconcerted he saw that the men were in singlets and knee-length shorts. Jemadar Lalitbahadur Gurung, who was in charge of the run that morning, saluted without seeming to notice any difference in Paul's attire. Just too bad, Paul thought to himself. Anyway, he had a good athletic figure and was very fit. He ran the three miles without discomfort, which the Gurkhas noted with interest.

Later, after Paul had changed into uniform, Martin took him to meet Lieutenant-Colonel Butterworth. The colonel was a tall, slightly built man, with dark eyes and lean face, and a thin black moustache. He was a bachelor yet married to the regiment. For more than twenty years he had been a good husband and a good father, worshipped by the men, loved in that special sexless fashion that men like the Gurkhas can feel towards a select few. He knew them all, not just those in the present battalion, but throughout the regiment, and their fathers and uncles and brothers and cousins who may have served at some time during those years. He could speak the language fluently. The old cliché that his men would lay down their lives for him was true. And they knew that he would lay down his life for them.

Butterworth had been given the task of raising the 5th Battalion only a few months earlier, with insufficient officers and few men. And now they had sent him an American. No! No! he rebuked himself. He had to keep an open mind. And when Paul marched in and saluted, the colonel felt like heaving a sigh of relief. At least the young man was presentable, smart and well-spoken; his years at an English university and in the British Army probably accounted for a lessening of the American accent. And the colonel, who knew everything that went on his battalion, was aware that Paul had immediately involved himself in battalion life by going on the run that morning.

'Which part of America do you come from?' he asked.

'New York, sir.'

'Well that's a change.' The colonel smiled. 'I thought all Americans came from Texas.'

Paul did not realize that the light-hearted banter was a compliment to him. Behind the mask of confidence, when Paul first entered the colonel's office he had been shit-scared! But something about the colonel told him he need not be so apprehensive. All the same, he was relieved when it was over and that the experience had not been more frightening. It never occurred to him that his own character and appearance had been responsible for his acceptance by the colonel. And when he met more of the officers at lunch in the Mess he was again surprised at the lack of anti-American feeling. He was just the new junior officer, being put at ease where possible, but kept at just sufficient distance to remind him that he was a second-lieutenant.

After lunch, Martin told him: '*Diwali* is a holiday for the men. They can do more or less what they want. There'll probably be a poker school going.'

Paul looked quickly at the captain. Was this the first knock at him for being an American? Were the gloves coming off in the insinuation that Americans were crazy about poker?

Martin laughed, 'The Gurkhas love all card games.'

'But, poker, sir?'

'Oh that's easily explained. The Gurkha and the British Tommy have always been great friends, and that's how our men were initiated into the art of poker. But, look here, I'm going to be tied up with the Subedar Sahib on some promotion mix-up, so what would you like to do? Go around the company with Lalitbahadur and get to meet some of the men, perhaps. It's a good way of picking up the language.'

From his vantage point in the 15 Platoon hut, Naik Amarjit Limbu saw Paul approaching with Jemadar Lalitbahadur. 'Here is the American Sahib,' said Amarjit. The three Gurkhas playing poker with him looked up from the cards for the moment.

'He is a very good runner – very fit,' Lance-Naik Bombahadur commented.

'What else do we know about him?' Rifleman Jangbir queried.

'Not much,' Rifleman Kamansing suggested.

'Americans are supposed to be very good at poker,' Amarjit said. 'Perhaps we should ask him to join us.'

'But if he is so good . . .' Bombahadur started to protest.

Amarjit interrupted him. 'He can only be as good as he is allowed to be. It is quite easy, we will just tell each other what cards we have in our hands. He will not understand, and we shall have a good idea of what cards he has.'

Jangbir was nervous. Amarjit placated him. 'It will only be

for fun.'

'You mean we will not play for money?'

'Of course we must play for money otherwise it would not be so interesting.'

'But to play for money with an officer sahib, and to cheat him – why we could be in very serious trouble.'

Bombahadur, who was also not happy, suggested. 'Perhaps if we return his losses it might not be so bad.'

'All right, that is what we will do.' The others did not trust him to do so, but kept quiet. Kamansing, however, did raise the point. 'What about the Jemadar Sahib?'

'He will not interfere,' Amarjit said haughtily. They all knew that Lalitbahadur was nervous and rather slack.

As Paul approached the hut, Amarjit called the men to attention. 'Carry on,' said Paul in English. He climbed the steps into the hut. At once he could sense Amarjit's hostility, even hatred, and he wondered what the cause was because it was so unlike the cheerfulness and friendliness shown by the other Gurkhas. Paul did not know that Amarjit was a wealthy young man, heir to estates in Darjeeling which in itself made him unique as the vast majority of Gurkha soldiers came from very poor families, and looked upon their pay, which was ludicrously meagre, yet more than they would have earned in Nepal, as a moderate means of support for their families now, and themselves in old age. Every Gurkha soldier supported at least five members of his family back in Nepal.

Amarjit was a clean-limbed young man in his early twenties, somewhat fairer than the other men, and his features were not so Mongolian. There had been no need for him to join the army, but he had been drawn in by a craving for adventure and to emulate his father, a World War I hero. The other Gurkhas treated him with a mixture of respect, awe and fear because of his intelligence and wealth; but they also were certain that one day his pride would lead him into serious trouble.

'Sahib play cards?' Amarjit asked in broken English although he knew that no Gurkha was supposed to speak English to an officer, but only Gurkhali to ensure that he learnt the language. There was also the added insult, of which Paul was unaware, that in fact Amarjit could speak English fluently, having attended St Paul's School in Darjeeling.

56

Paul glanced at the jemadar who made no response. Perhaps it was all right for an officer to play cards with the men. 'Why not?' said Paul, taking off his Gurkha hat.

'Sahib sit here.' Amarjit pointed to the place by his side and Paul squatted on his haunches like the men. Around them the oil lamps lit for *Diwali*, brightened the drabness of the barracks hut.

'We play for one pice,' Amarjit said, holding up the coin which had the least value in Indian currency. He also explained that the maximum bet at any time would be two pice.

Paul's instinct warned him that he should not be playing cards with the men for money, but when he looked at Lalitbahadur again for guidance, the jemadar remained silent, and the young American decided that it must be all right.

In Gurkhali, Amarjit said, 'We will let him win the first hand.' The others kept their eyes down, not happy about the situation, but too afraid to challenge Amarjit.

They started to play, and according to plan Paul won the first hand. But not according to plan he also won the second, third and fourth – the last one on two pairs – and threw in his hand early in the fifth.

Amarjit's features were drawn with anger and confusion as he dealt the cards for the sixth hand. Paul had a pair of kings, and opened for one pice – he had deliberately kept the betting as low as possible. The others stayed in for the same amount, Amarjit having great difficulty in keeping his face blank because he had dealt himself a full house of aces and queens. In a matter of fact voice he told the other what he had. 'This time we will get him,' he added.

When it came to the draw, Paul asked for three cards. Bombahadur discarded one, Jangbir and Kamansing three each. Amarjit stuck to his original hand.

Paul opened the betting with one pice. Bombahadur hesitated. 'Well, what have you got?' Amarjit snapped.

'I think this has gone too far,' Bombahadur said nervously.

'It is too late now – we have got him.'

'Just two pairs,' Bombahadur said, and dropped out of the game. But the cards he had placed face down in front of him included four jacks.

'If you do not stay in the game we will not be able to raise the bet high enough,' Amarjit said angrily.

'I only have three sevens,' said Jangbir, 'and I am not going on in this hand.'

'Neither am I,' said Kamansing.

'Cowards,' Amarjit turned to Paul, 'One pice and,' he took out a five rupee note which had been tucked into the corner of his shorts, 'and Sahib play big money?'

Paul hesitated, then said firmly, 'No. Two pice limit.'

Amarjit sneered openly much to the other Gurkhas' horror and shame. He said in Gurkhali: 'And these American Sahibs are supposed to be so rich and such mad, daring gamblers.'

Amarjit raised the bet by two pice, and Paul met it to call him. With a flourish, Amarjit laid down his full house and reached out for the pot only to find his wrist held firmly by the American. There was no great pressure, but Amarjit could sense the strength, and knew that he would not be able to move if he tried.

'Not so fast,' Paul said, showing the four kings in his hand.

Amarjit tugged furiously, trying to break free, and Paul released his wrist. 'I think I'll call it a day,' the American said, standing up to leave, the others rising with him. The jemadar heaved a sigh of relief as did Amarjit's poker friends.

Paul had the winnings in his hand – they did not amount to much. Was now the time to play that ace up his sleeve? The ace dealt him by his room-mate at Bangalore – Prem Senna, the Nepalese from Kathmandu, intelligent, a fine young man who was not permitted to take a commission in a Gurkha regiment – which in those days only accepted British officers – but would have to join an Indian unit. In the six months at OTS it had been fairly simple for a linguist like Paul, fresh from university, to learn Prem's language. Prem had also given him a copy of Captain Money's famous *Gurkhali Manual*: while the three months at the Regimental Centre had provided the final touch.

Now Paul looked at Jemadar Lalitbahadur and said in fluent Gurkhali: 'I am not sure if I should keep this money, Jemadar Sahib.'

Lalitbahadur began to say, 'Well, Sahib –' when he stopped abruptly, realizing that he had been addressed in his own language. His mouth suddenly fell open.

'I am not accustomed to playing men's games with children,' Paul said. 'Especially children who cheat.'

Naik Amarjit stood straight, face drawn in nervousness. 'The Sahib cheated by not telling us he spoke our language.'

'Keep quiet!' Bombahadur snarled. 'Have you not done enough harm already? You have brought shame to our platoon.'

'Were you so innocent then?'

'No. I was weak. And the shame is mine also.'

Then, in typical Gurkha fashion, a rifleman at the back of the hut saved the situation. 'Ay – the Sahib was too clever for you. Fancy telling him what cards you had in your hands!' He began to laugh, followed by another, and soon all members of the platoon, apart from Amarjit, were in fits of laughter, doubled up, tears streaming down their faces (evidence of the Gurkhas' great sense of humour).

Men from C Company's 13 and 14 platoons came running to find out what was the matter. And when told, they too held their sides. There had not been a jape like this in a long time, and it was a tale to savour for years and no doubt to embellish and pass into the unwritten history of the regiment.

Lieutenant-Colonel Butterworth, strolling through the battalion lines with the subedar-major, wondered what was causing the disturbance in C Company. Then he saw a small figure running through the trees. 'Lalsing!'

The battalion's youngest member halted abruptly and froze to attention. 'Come here, child,' the colonel beckoned.

Lalsing ran forward. The subedar-major growled, 'Well, tell the Colonel Sahib.' If there was any gossip to be passed around the battalion it was always little Lalsing who spread the word.

He told the colonel, trying to stop his shoulders from shaking with mirth, eyes sparkling in his cherubic face. The colonel, finding it difficult to keep his features severe said, 'All right. Off you go.' The diminutive figure disappeared swiftly through the trees. 'What shall we do Subedar-Major

59

Sahib?'

Officially, in the 15th, gambling is allowed only at *Diwali* as it is an integral part of the festival, and the Gurkhas are such avid gamblers that they make the most of the privilege. This time, however, an officer was involved.

'Amarjit has always been a problem, Colonel Sahib,' the subedar-major replied after a slight pause. 'So full of pride and difficult to handle. No doubt he could be a very good soldier. And now it seems that he has found his master at last! So I would suggest, Sahib, that for someone like him the humiliation has been much more severe than any punishment we could inflict.'

The colonel agreed. 'It seems that our American Sahib is going to give us a few surprises.'

☆　☆　☆

In the C Company lines Paul said to Lalitbahadur, 'I have no intention of returning this money. But I think that it should suffice to buy cigarettes for the company?'

Lalitbahadur grinned, 'Yes, Sahib.'

Paul stepped closer to the jemadar and spoke softly, 'By the way, Jemadar Sahib, you knew what was going on, but made no attempt to stop it. It seems to me that you are afraid of the men.'

A startled Lalitbahadur said nervously, 'No, Sahib! I knew it was a game, a bit of fun.'

'I do not think that was the way Amarjit saw it. I may not be a British officer, but I intend to be as good as one, if not better. If you do not wish to find yourself returned to the Regimental Centre, you will have to show a great improvement in your handling of the men, in the running of your platoon. I shall be keeping a very close eye on you. That is all.'

'Yes, Sahib. I . . . I will do as you say.' Then he snapped to attention and called the company to order in a tone that had not been heard from him for a long time. The laughter stopped, everyone stood to attention.

The jemadar saluted. Paul returned the salute, turned and walked away, his heart beating quite fast, his legs feeling shaky. It was always like this after a period of conflict and tension.

Behind him someone shouted, '*Shabash!* American Sahib!' And there were loud cheers. But he did not look back. He knew that he had been accepted into the battalion.

Wait Till You Nod Your Head

Under cover of darkness, the Gurkha patrol came silently across no man's land towards the German trenches. Ready to hand were their kukris, the national weapon – a heavy knife, honed to a sharpness that could remove a man's head from his shoulders with one stroke. It was some seventeen inches long from the top of the handle to the pointed tip of the twelve inch, broad, angled blade.

Moving stealthily past the shell holes, the dead, the pockets of tangled wire, freezing for a moment as a flare lit up the night, the patrol reached the German trenches and dropped suddenly out of the darkness, in among the enemy, using their kukris with deadly effect.

Indeed, so quick and efficient were they that one German soldier said to a Gurkha who had engaged him in close combat: 'Ah! You missed me.'

The Gurkha grinned.

'Wait till you nod your head,' he said.

Gurkha's Road

By the afternoon Girbahadur was still alive. But of the Gurkha section which had defended the position astride the rough, dirt road, only his eyes looked out into this world.

The small band of Gurkhas had fought tenaciously throughout the long, dark night and into the light of day until the Japs had withdrawn in confusion, leaving a silence broken only by the buzzing of flies gathering quickly among the corpses.

Although Girbahadur was wounded, and all alone, he was not afraid. He knew there was only a slight chance that help from the battalion would reach him before the Japs, having licked their wounds, attacked again. But he would be ready, and that was why he was not afraid.

His last grenade was concealed beneath his body, a finger crooked through the ring of the safety pin. He would take a few Japs with him when he pulled out the pin. But what a pity, he thought, that the battalion would never know of his practical joke. When he imagined the expressions on the Japs' faces in that instant before death, he laughed aloud.

His cracked lips smarted as he did so; his mouth was afire with thirst. He had lost his hat during one of the sharp hand-to-hand clashes and the sun was fierce on his shaven head, perspiration trickling into his eyes. Several hours of torment lay ahead before the sun would be low enough for the dry, blackened bamboos to cast a cool shadow over the slit trench. He could crawl over to the scant shelter of the bamboo forest now, but that, he considered, would be tantamount to desertion.

So he lay in the trench and thought of his home, of the snow on the Himalayas, and the brisk winds blowing through the valleys. In the summer, when the snow-line was higher and the afternoon sun was hot, there was always the *duramsala*, a stone shelter built at the side of the road for weary travellers to rest in its shady interior. He wished that there was one at the side of this road.

The sun grew hotter and Girbahadur's eyes closed with the glare. Then suddenly he did not feel the heat any more. His head was cool, his mouth fresh with enough spittle to spit across the road, while his bare feet and hands welcomed the invigorating touch of cold stone. He wondered why his feet were bare – what had happened to his boots? And how did the trench suddenly have a stone floor? He opened his eyes and found that he was sitting in the *duramsala* near his home in Nepal, and at his side was his friend Tulbir.

Girbahadur rubbed his eyes in bewilderment. Which was the dream? The jungles of Burma, or the valley and mountains of his home? He looked down at himself. He was not in uniform now, but wore long, white trousers, close-fitting from the ankles to just above the knees, then widening out like jodhpurs. His short, black jacket was dirty and torn. Perched on the back of his head was a skull cap beneath which his black hair was thick and long. (Back in those days as soon as a Gurkha joined the army his head was shaven).

He turned to his friend, and was about to speak to him when he noticed old Subedar Padamsing Rai approaching, his walking-stick tapping on the cobblestones.

When the subedar travelled down to the Recruiting Centre at Ghoom, near Darjeeling, to collect his pension, he always tried to take with him a few young Gurkhas eager to join the army. The British Raj, in its benevolence, had granted him a pension for the long years of loyal service through the smoke of many battles. But the Raj's benevolence was far from generous and the subedar had to supplement his budget by the few rupees commission he received for bringing in likely recruits. Now, seeing the two youths, and having appraised their value, he sat down beside them in the shade of the *duramsala*.

Padamsing still looked every inch a soldier. His back was straight, and in his voice there remained the authoritative command of the parade ground. In his dress he tried to maintain some semblance of a uniform. Although his trousers were in the native style, his well-worn service jacket bristled with old campaign medals and the decoration he cherished – the IOM (Indian Order of Merit) won on the North-West Frontier some decades past. To his black, pill-box hat was affixed the regimental badge of the 15th Gurkha Rifles, the silver crossed-kukris polished till they reflected like heliographs. His hair was close-cropped, and his moustache, although grey, was waxed to fine points.

Twisting his moustache out of habit, he pointed his stick and asked: 'Do you know who donated this *duramsala*?'

Girbahadur answered, 'Subedar-Major Gaje Rai.'

'That is right,' Padamsing nodded his head. 'I knew him well. We fought side by side in the Great War when he won many distinctions, and became an honorary lieutenant. He was about your age when he joined the army. Who would have guessed that one day he would be a subedar-major and win the Victoria Cross. Of course I do not have a soothsayer's powers, but one of you might well be destined for similar honours.'

'I have often thought of joining up,' Girbahadur said innocently.

The subedar inspected him like a farmer looking over a goat before taking it to market. Here was a most likely recruit. 'Then you should join. It is the life for a man, so thrilling, adventurous. I travelled across vast seas in a great ship, and saw many wondrous things. I earned lots of money, ate well and grew strong. Now in my old age I wish for youth so that I may live through those days again.'

The trenches near Festubert returned vividly to his mind; finding those parapets so high that the men could not look over the top and had to make fire-steps from sandbags and planks, and the trenches so full of water that some of the smallest Gurkhas were drowned in the night. And he remembered his first experience of the full blast of modern artillery, of comrades blown to smithereens, of wounded suffocated beneath the soggy debris of broken parapets. And he remembered the wire at Loos, not cut by the artillery barrage, and how the dead of the 1st Battalion piled up four or five deep as the Gurkhas sought desperately for a way through to get to grips with the Germans whose machine-guns were savaging the brave ranks of the battalion. Well, they had got to grips with the enemy, and used their kukris as savagely as the machine-guns, and he remembered the German youth, crying and screaming like a woman as he brought his already blood-stained kukri down and across the exposed neck. But these were memories he could not share with these young Gurkhas. A new war had broken out, so it was said in the bazaar, and they would learn the truth in good time. Now let them be fattened like the goat for market, on the glory and the glamour.

'Come with me to Ghoom when I go to draw my pension. You will never regret it.'

Girbahadur thought of his father, and the other men of the village, breaking their backs trying to eke out a livelihood on the rugged, terraced fields. And like a great many young men before him he could see the Indian Army as a passport out of the valley, and a means to support his family.

'I will enlist,' he committed himself impulsively; and because Tulbir was Girbahadur's devoted friend, he too said he would join the army.

Just before the end of the month they accompanied Padamsing and three more volunteers on the journey to Ghoom. It was a long time since the subedar had enticed so many recruits, and he was aware that the outbreak of the new war was the obvious attraction. And not just the war, but the knowledge that the quota of recruits for the Gurkha regiments would be increased considerably, and more spaces meant more chance of being selected, and more mouths fed back in Nepal.

The old subedar felt a spring in his step, already day-dreaming about the extra commission that would come his way, increasing all the time as the war with an insatiable appetite like some ravenous beast would draw more and still more young men from the hills.

All day they followed the winding road down the steep hillsides, past terraced fields and small hamlets, through occasional arbours where the sun's rays slanted off the tree trunks and green, springy moss covered the cobblestones. Miles and miles of hill ranges and valleys, green with trees and blood-red with rhododendrons, rolled away to the snowy mountains which towered above them in white majesty. Far below a river twisted and turned along the route carved out through the ages and sparkled in the sun.

The Gurkhas walked steadily on with the springy stride of hillmen, Padamsing leading the way to set a pace to suit his age. All he carried was his stick, while the recruits carried their own few belongings. But at the rear was a little Gurkha porter, weighed down with a huge basket on his back containing the subedar's luggage which seemed excessive for so short a trip. A cloth band attached to the basket was pulled over the porter's head and stretched across his forehead to help him carry the load.

No one spoke, but Tulbir sang. He had a good voice, the words of the love songs echoing around the hills, telling of the girl from Naini Tal; and of the girl from Kalimpong and the squeaking of her new shoes. And then he sang the sad *Gurkha's Road:*

> *Bachyo bhane, yo bato aula,*
> *Maryo bhane, baluwa sirane.*

It was a farewell to a loved one, and Girbahadur wondered what his fate would be. Like the words of the song, would he live to return along this road, or would he travel no further than six feet under the ground? He remembered leaving home that morning and walking past the house next door where Sainli had looked shyly out of her window. He remembered her oval face and small, flat nose, and her jet black hair parted in the middle and fastened in a knot at the back of her head with a little border of flowers. Their dark eyes had met and he had checked his stride, then she had turned coyly away. Even now he could feel the dryness in his mouth, the warmth that tingled in his loins. When he returned, he would marry Sainli. He had forgotten the words of *Gurkha's Road.*

That night the travellers were given a rough shelter in a hamlet where Padamsing had relations, and went to bed after a meal which left them feeling hungry, But it was a new adventure, and the excitement made up for the hunger.

Next day they continued for several hours through the foothills along the cobblestone track, halting for the second night at a roadside tavern – a small, wooden house with a mud floor and rickety tables. Padamsing was well-known to Jethi, the motherly, friendly woman who owned the tavern, and the young Gurkhas fed well that night.

The following morning they resumed their journey, making not too early a start because the subedar's head was in a delicate state after a night of hard drinking – a sort of pre-celebration of the largess to come. But it was only a short step from the tavern, and soon they passed Ghoom Monastery and the shanties where the charcoal fires blazed brightly as the knife makers forged kukris of all shapes and sizes.

The track brought them out onto the main Siliguri-Darjeeling road which shared its tarmac with a two feet gauge railway track. The young Gurkhas stared with open mouths. They had never travelled so far from their homes, and it was the first time that they had ever seen motor vehicles. Of course they had heard stories from travellers passing through the village, and returning soldiers, but had never really believed the tales of carts moving without the assistance of bullocks.

Suddenly a chilling scream echoed through the hills and across the deep valleys, making the young men jump with fright. Padamsing put his hands on his hips and doubled up with laughter, even though the scream had pierced his delicate head. 'Heh! Heh! It is the terrain, you country bumpkins!'

Some 9,000 feet below Ghoom, at the foot of the Eastern Himalayas, the main line from Calcutta ended at Siliguri. Passengers for the hill station of Darjeeling changed there to a miniature train which consisted of a small, squat locomotive – a pigmy beside *The Calcutta Mail* – but powerful enough to pull several carriages on the climb from the jungle to the pine forest.

From Siliguri the track followed the winding motor road, at times like a spiral staircase as it climbed, first through tropical jungle, next into deciduous forest and finally twisting and turning along the hairpin bends which hugged the mountain-sides, up through the pine forests which seemed to reach up to the sky. Now snow-capped peaks formed a pattern along the distant horizon, and far below, for mile upon mile, the land rolled away into the hazy plain of Bengal.

A loud puff-puff-puff signalled the approach of *The Darjeeling Mail,* and then it came into view, two men sitting on the front of the engine to drop sand on the rails to stop the train from slipping backwards on the steeper gradients.

Girbahadur had never seen a train before so this miniature railway did not seem small, but rather some mechanical monster puffing out steam like the dragons on the prayer flags in the temple.

At Ghoom, the highest point, the train followed a gigantic loop round the edge of a spur because of the gradient, before descending some 1,000 feet to Darjeeling, while the 28,000 feet Mt Kanchenjunga towered above in a block of snow and ice looking like a huge armchair.

When the train had passed out of sight, Padamsing led his wonder-struck recruits across the road and railway line, moving quickly, fearful of being run over by the cars and lorries which seemed to approach so suddenly and rush past with a roar of engines and a whine of wheels, the wind swirling behind them.

'Come along, come along!' the subedar said testily, 'Do you want everyone to see what yokels you are? And let me tell you, these are but small wonders to what await you in the world outside.'

They followed a footpath which wound like a corkscrew from the road, through the towering pine forest, then gradually levelled out until they reached the Recruiting Centre nestling among the trees. Padamsing led them to a long barrack full of raw recruits. 'You will stay here until you have been medically examined and inspected by the recruiting officers. I will return in due course.' Leaving them to pass the time as they may, he drifted off in search of old friends among the other pensioners who had gathered in Ghoom like members of some convention.

In the barracks some of the young Gurkhas were, like Girbahadur, awed by the suddenness of the new environment, and sat quietly amidst a murmur of voices, reflecting on the wonders they had already seen or feeling homesick for the familiar surroundings of the villages where time had stood still. The majority of the Gurkhas in the barracks came from Eastern Nepal, home of the Rais and Limbus, the tribes mostly recruited in the 7th and 10th Gurkha Rifles; the 15th took a proportion because it recruited men from most of the tribes.

Nepal is inhabited by many tribes. Just as in the United Kingdom there are the English, Welsh, Scots and Irish – or

69

broken down further into Yorkshireman, Lancastrian, Cornishman and the like – so from the western and central areas come the Thapas and Gurungs. In the Nepal Valley live the Khas or Chettri, recruited mainly in the 9th Gurkhas. Within the major clans are numerous branches, such as Ranas, Puns and Khandkas. and the Gurkha always adds his *clan* to his given name: like Girbahadur *Limbu*, or Padamsing *Rai* or Tekbahadur *Thapa*.

During a war of such magnitude as World War II, the demand is so great that regiments are often forced to accept men from tribes they would not normally consider.

After a successful medical examination, Girbahadur and Tulbir with about thirty other young men, stripped to their loincloths, assembled on the parade ground. A cold wind blew across the mountains and fanned Girbahadur's body. He shuffled his feet impatiently while the recruiting officer and his staff passed slowly along the ranks. But presently the officer reached Girbahadur, and his blue, friendly eyes calmed the young Gurkha's nervousness.

The officer made a comment to his assistant who, with a piece of white chalk, wrote the figure 15 on Girbahadur's bare back to indicate that he would be enrolled in the 15th Gurkha Rifles. Girbahadur knew that the numeral had been written on his back because he could see it quite clearly.

But how could he see his own back? He felt perspiration prick his skin and he trembled with fright. The chalk mark grew larger and larger, then it broke into hundreds of fifteens. And the parade ground and the recruiting officer and the recruits began to whirl round and round, faster and faster like a giant wheel until they all jumbled together in a black, whirling mass. Then the wheel disintegrated, and there was only the trench and the bamboos and the night.

Slowly Girbahadur regained control of his senses. He felt quite weak, and his wound had started to throb again. It was cooler in the trench now that darkness had fallen, but the spittle had dried in his mouth and his tongue felt swollen and sore. He still trembled as his delirium had been so real.

Suddenly he grew alert. What was that? Somebody had moved out there in the darkness. His finger tightened around the safety pin of the grenade. Another sound – of a small stone rolling over. The Japs! He pulled the pin but it did not move.

70

He tried again, tugging with all his remaining strength, but still without success. Then he swore softly as he realized that he had forgotten to straighten the splayed ends of the pin.

But as his fingers started frantically to press the two metal ends together so that the pin could be released something stopped them. Somebody had spoken out there, and it was not in Japanese. There it was again: 'They are all dead, Sahib.'

Girbahadur tried to call out but his vocal cords refused to work, and the shout that would not pass his lips resounded in his mind. He made another desperate attempt, and this time managed a croaking, 'Here! I am here!'

Then two figures bent over the slit trench, and strong, but gentle hands lifted him out. The British officer, speaking softly, said, 'Well done, Girbahadur. We will soon have you away from this place.'

Girbahadur relaxed. Now that the major sahib had arrived he knew that everything would be all right. He was hoisted onto a strong back and carried to safety.

They had not gone far when they heard mortar bombs exploding behind them. The enemy had delayed too long. But Girbahadur was not interested in bombs. The fireflies in the darkness ahead were like the lights of Darjeeling, and he was thinking of Sainli who would be waiting at the end of the road.

The Hill Runner

When Captain Finch broke his leg they carried him down the hillside, and the whole battalion watched in silence as the stretcher-bearers slowly negotiated the steep slope.

There was despair on every face without exception, because Finch was one of the few British officers who could match the Gurkha in a *Khud Race* – the annual Hill Race which called for great skill and courage, hurtling down 1,000 feet of precipitous ground strewn with sharp-edged rocks, great boulders and rough tussock-grass. It was during a practice run that Finch had misjudged a giant leap and collided with a boulder, and so he was being carried down on the stretcher, out of this year's race, and probably never to participate again.

'What are we going to do?' Lieutenant-Colonel Brent of the 2/15th Gurkhas asked of his adjutant, Captain Steele.

'I've been racking my brains, sir, trying to think of a replacement. There's Jones . . . .'

'Oh, no! What about Jackson, Welham – yes, you may well shake your head. Peters – he's athletic, isn't he?'

'He was, sir,' Steele said. 'I'm afraid he has rather allowed himself to go to seed.'

The colonel was in despair. 'We'll have to scratch. And God knows what the Brigadier will say.' Or even not say, he thought to himself, which was usually a lot worse.

'Well, perhaps something will turn up. Let's look on the bright side.'

The expression on his face did not hold out much promise of success within the three days left for the big race.

The tradition of *khud* racing in the Indian Army had its roots in 1890 with the holding of the first race which was to become an annual event. It was also good training for getting men down quickly from the North-West Frontier piquets.

There were 133 starters that day, and the first thirty-three places were won by Gurkhas; a domination maintained over the next twenty-five years until the First World War when the race was shelved.

The event was not revived until 1931, and the original rules were changed. Instead of an individual event, it became a relay race, with each team consisting of eight men who ran in pairs. There were four legs, two uphill, two down, and the first man of each pair to arrive at the change-over released both runners for the next leg.

But there was one brigade in India which had organised its own event, run under its own rules – a typical example, as everyone in the Indian Army knew, of that brigadier's insular outlook and snobbishness. This was a charge with which its commander, Brigadier Peterson, would have violently disagreed if anyone were so bold as to raise the matter with him.

The point was that it showed originality, the brigadier defended himself. And originality, determination, accepting responsibility would, he believed, be important ingredients in World War II which he always forecast as just beyond the horizon.

Under his rules, each team consisted of one officer and five men. Points were awarded according to the position each man in the team finished. First would be one point, seventh would be seven points. Fiftieth would be fifty points and so on. And the team with the lowest score was the winner. If any member of the team failed to complete the course there was an automatic 120 points penalty.

The field was restricted to twenty teams, and the race was thrown open to all comers. Although the brigade was criticised for its independence, there was no shortage of applications from just about every regiment in India. The final selection was always a cross-section of the Indian Army – British, Punjabis, Mahrattas, Sikhs, Jats, Rajputs, Dogras, Gurkhas, Baluchis and many others.

And in the three years since the race had been launched in 1932, one of Peterson's own brigade teams had always been the winner. It was the team led by Captain Finch of the 2/15th.

But it seemed that 1935 would be a disaster year. Brigadier

Peterson was a man who forgot nothing and forgave little, and the possibility of a winner from outside his brigade was too horrible to contemplate.

Lieutenant-Colonel Brent gave an involuntary shudder, then stood up abruptly behind his desk, picking up his field hat and swagger stick. 'Let's go and see how poor old Finch is getting on,' he said to the adjutant. They left Battalion Headquarters and entered the staff car which was waiting to take them on the thirty mile drive to the Army General Hospital.

The journey was completed in silence, each man going over the list of probables again and again in his head, and discarding each candidate with equal finality. They were no closer to a decision when the driver turned into the grounds of the hospital.

They climbed the stairs to the first floor where the sister said, 'Don't stay very long, please. And try not to overtax him – he's still rather weak.'

The colonel grunted, the adjutant gave the sister a hard stare which she ignored as she was quite used to dealing with officers of the highest rank.

Captain Finch was in a private room, his leg in plaster raised in a cradle. Above him a fan rotated in its battle against the blistering heat. Finch looked pale despite his deep tan, and his face seemed to have shrivelled in the short time since he had broken his leg.

Brent coughed and Finch opened his eyes. 'Colonel,' he murmured.

'My boy. How are you? Being well looked after, I hope?' He sat down in a cane armchair, feeling uncomfortable. He disliked visiting hospitals although, as colonel of the battalion, it was a task he had to perform quite often. Captain Steele stood by the window, trying to take advantage of the faint breath of cool air that struggled limply across the window-ledge.

'The race,' Finch said, his voice almost a croak.

'Don't worry about it,' the colonel tried to soothe him.

'Fisher,' Finch said softly.

'Fisher!' exclaimed the colonel.

'Fisher?' repeated the adjutant, stepping up to the bed, not sure if he had heard correctly.

The colonel looked at his adjutant, their eyes meeting in disbelief. They turned back to Finch. 'Did you say Fisher?' the colonel asked. But Finch seemed to have fallen asleep.

'Finch,' the adjutant said. Then raised his voice, 'Finch!' And this brought the sister quickly into the room.

'I'm sorry. You must leave now.'

'But –' the adjutant began.

'You can see he's exhausted,' she interrupted firmly. He needs plenty of rest, poor chap, after all he's been through.'

The officers retreated, and spent the whole of the return journey in silence; each man's thoughts on the race, but this time thinking only of Fisher.

Meanwhile Second-Lieutenant Trevor Fisher, blissfully unaware of the pending changes looming into his life, sat alone in his tent, listening to Chopin on a portable gramophone. The fact that he was alone was a significant pointer to his introvertive nature. Although he had been with the battalion for almost six months he had made no real friend. But, to be fair, it was not his fault. The truth was that he had been accepted into the battalion under sufferance.

He did not have the look of an officer of the 15th Gurkha Rifles. At twenty-one he was short, swarthy, thin with black unruly hair, a lean face to match his leanness, and his uniform seemed to hang on him. He was close to being *scruffy*.

Yet he should have been the perfect officer because the Fishers had been represented from the day the 15th was raised. His grandfather, father, an uncle and several cousins had all made the name Fisher synonymous with the regiment. Trevor, himself, had been brought up in the lines, when his father commanded the 1st Battalion before going on to get his brigade. His grandfather had retired as General Sir Peter Fisher.

The young Fisher could speak Gurkhali more fluently than English, and before he had reached his teens knew more about the character of the men than any officer. And by the time he was fourteen he could run with the best of them across the Himalayan foothills. Eventually and reluctantly he left for England to finish his education, and at twenty-one he had returned to the regiment to continue the Fisher tradition.

He was an immediate disappointment, but with such a

pedigree could not be refused. 'If we give him enough rope perhaps he'll hang himself,' Brent said longingly when he was forced to accept Trevor into the 2nd Battalion. Being so prejudiced, the colonel and his adjutant would never have considered him for the *Khud Race* team, but Captain Finch, as Trevor's company commander, knew his background, knew that behind the uninviting exterior was a real *pahari*, a man of the hills, a British officer who had breathed the same air as the Gurkhas, was one with them. Such a background was too strong not to be used to advantage, Finch had decided as he lay in the hospital bed trying not to despair at the tragedy of his broken leg. It would be a great opportunity for young Fisher, and really the battalion's only chance.

'Let's get it over,' the colonel said when they returned to Battalion HQ, and an orderly was despatched to summon Trevor, who arrived a few minutes later wondering what he had done wrong on this occasion.

'Ah . . . er . . . Fish . . . er . . . Trevor,' the colonel began, an approach which put Fisher more on his guard. 'We've just been to see Captain Finch.'

'Oh! How was he, sir?' Trevor asked, showing more interest.

'I'm afraid he won't be up and about for a long time,' the colonel said. 'And very depressed, poor fellow, at missing the *Khud Race*. Feels he's let the side down.'

'But it was a pure accident,' Trevor protested.

'Quite. But that's not the way he sees it. Anyway, his main concern is for the battalion team.' The colonel paused, finding it difficult to bring out the words, especially with Trevor standing more like a farmer than a soldier, and he had not even bothered to comb his hair. 'The fact is, he thought that you should take his place in the race. I presume you have had previous experience?'

'Yes, sir,' Trevor said, showing no sign of emotion.

'Well, what about it?' Brent half hoped that Trevor would refuse, and provide the rope he had been waiting for.

'Is that an order, sir?'

'Yes!' the colonel snapped before he had time to consider his reply.

'Very well, sir,' Fisher confirmed.

When he had left the office, the adjutant said explosively,

'He's a cold one!'

Brent shook his head in doubt. 'I've always had a great respect for Finch's ability, but I fear that this will turn out to be an error of judgment.'

Back in his tent Trevor was trembling with fright – if the adjutant could have seen him he would have been horrified at the change. 'My God! What will I do?' Trevor said aloud. Of all the misfortunes that had befallen him, this time fate had really excelled.

He sat back in his camp-chair, eyes closed, feeling the perspiration breaking out in his armpits and across his forehead. Why had he not refused? He had already put up so many blacks he had been afraid to say no, and now he was really in deep trouble, and it could only end in disgrace when he was branded a coward.

Yes, he had been a hill runner, and a very good one, but he had not run since that fateful day when Dilbahadur and he were out on the Himalayan foothills – an English boy and his young Gurkha friend, one the son of a battalion colonel, the other of its subedar-major.

As they trotted along the ridge they could see the Regimental Centre in the distance, laid out in neat squares, red roofs through the pines. Dilbahadur looked at Trevor and grinned, teeth white and even in his round, cheerful face. 'I will get there before you, Treever!'

'Do you want a start, Dillee?'

'From an old man.' Dilbahadur sped down the slope in leaps and bounds, followed by Trevor. Half way down he had almost caught up with the Gurkha, but the ground to the right fell away in a long drop, and Dilbahadur, without hesitation, launched himself into the void.

'Dillee!' Trevor shouted, but too late.

He watched the Gurkha boy descend, arms in the air, legs straight, swooping like a bird of prey. Dillee's feet hit the ground and at first Trevor thought he had made the jump, but then he saw him wobble and fall sprawling, scattering the pine-cones in all directions, his voice coming back up the hill in a long drawn out 'Treever!' as he rolled over and crashed into a pine tree.

'Dillee!' Trevor screamed. 'Dillee!' The Gurkha boy lay still. Trevor was about to jump down when he stopped abruptly, his legs shaking. He turned away and took the long route and when he reached Dilbahadur the young Gurkha was sitting up against the tree, and his eyes were open.

'Dillee. Thank God! You are safe,' Trevor cried out. But when he approached he could see that his friend's eyes were staring into nothing, and there was blood on his mouth. He touched Dilbahadur who fell forward. And then Trevor saw the back of the Gurkha's head, and he was violently sick.

'Sahib. Huzoor!' The voice returned him to the present. The tent was gloomy in the late evening. 'Yes, come in.'

As the uniformed figure entered the tent, Trevor called out, 'Dillee!'

'No, Sahib. Hastabir.'

'Hastabir. For a moment in the dark – '

'Dillee and I were said to be very much alike. And the Sahib awakening from a deep sleep in which, no doubt, he was dreaming . . . .'

'Yes, a dream. What did you want?'

'Shall I light the lamp?' Hastabir flicked up the glass of the oil-lamp and applied a match to the wick. Even in the light he was uncannily like his younger brother.

'You are taking Captain Finch Sahib's place, I understand.'

'Oh, of course, you are in the team.'

'I am the senior man, Sahib.' He paused, wondering how to phrase his next question. 'Is the Sahib in training for the race?'

It was tactfully put, Trevor thought. But his own reply was more direct. 'I have not been on a hill run since the day your brother died.'

'The race is in only three days' time.'

'I am not doing any training,' Trevor said firmly, but with a hint of desperation which Hastabir did not fail to notice. 'I might break a leg,' Trevor added in explanation.

'As the Sahib wishes,' the havildar said, but already he was afraid of what might happen on the day of the race, especially to Trevor. If the British officers were not very taken with Trevor, to the Gurkhas he was someone special. He was a Fisher, and none of the other officers could speak the language so fluently, or understand the Gurkhas' little ways.

'What about the tactics, Huzoor?'

'Had Finch Sahib made a plan?'

'We were to run together as a team uphill, then everyone for himself on the downhill section.'

'Then we will keep to his plan, Hastabir.'

Before dawn on the day of the race, a mass of spectators had gathered beneath the hill course, like a black, shapeless pool, ruffled by the murmur of voices, with an occasional ripple of laughter which seemed to increase the tension. Men of many nationalities, drawn from just about every type of military unit, they waited for daybreak when the race was to be run before the heat of the day became intolerable.

Now the sun was just nibbling at the hilltop, the gold edges tracing the line of the course. First an uphill stretch of about 1,000 feet, bare of vegetation; then a long slant to the top of the ridge for about half a mile; then the precipitous downhill section of 1,500 feet of sheer *khud*: sharp-edged rocks, great boulders, tussocks of rough grass. And the first men home were expected to complete the course in under fifteen minutes, taking only an incredible three and a half minutes to cover the downhill section.

Now more daylight was spreading across the course, and spectators and runners could be seen. In his black shorts and rifle green vest with the crossed-kukris motif of the 15th, Trevor shivered. He hoped it was only the cold of the early morning, and he glanced surreptitiously at his team gathered around him but they gave no indication that they had noticed. Indeed, it would have been entirely out of character for them to have done so.

Hastabir looked solid and dependable, and of the other four one was Dhanbahadur, easily the fastest Gurkha runner at that time, and next to him Budhiparsad, who was almost as fast. The remaining two were capable of finishing in the first thirty, as was Hastabir. But it would all be to no avail if Trevor failed to finish the course – the 120 penalty points would make sure of that.

Right on time the competitors were called into line. Without delay the starter fired his pistol, and as the 120 runners moved forward in a mass on the 1,000 feet uphill section, a great roar from the spectators echoed through the hills.

According to plan, Trevor and his men ran as a team, keeping to the same seemingly unhurried jog-trot, heads well down, hands put out occasionally to steady themselves, but climbing at well over 100 feet a minute. At this stage, some of the other nationalities, like the British and Punjabis, would have the advantage, but the race was usually won on the downhill section where the Gurkhas were almost impossible to beat.

Trevor could feel the strain on his muscles, but knew he would be able to keep going to the top. As a non-smoker who drank moderately, and with no excess fat, and the fact that he had always exercised, his lack of hill training had so far not proved to be a disability.

His Gurkhas were moving well, no sign of any discomfort, and presently they reached the long half a mile slant to the top of the ridge which called for bold running, striding out, upright now, despite the cruelly uneven surface. He glanced at his wrist-watch; they were on course to reach the top of the ridge in ten minutes. Although there were some teams ahead, he was confident they would all be overtaken on the downhill section.

But he had little confidence in his own ability. He had survived in the close company of his team as running to a pattern had for the moment lulled his fears. But now the top of the ridge was in sight, and beyond that he could picture the steep descent, dangerous as a minefield with its sharp rocks and boulders which took sheer guts and a perfect balance to avoid at high speed.

He could feel his heart beating quickly, his legs turning to jelly. I'll never do it! he thought. But he forced himself to keep moving until the top was reached.

'Go now!' he shouted, and Dhanbahadur and Budhiparsad seemed to step into space as they plunged down, followed closely by the other two. It was the moment the spectators had been waiting for, the thrilling sight of the leading Gurkhas hurtling down in great leaps, bounding from foothold to foothold. Maniraj of the 5th was there, and Pirtibahadur of the 6th using all their skill and courage to try and pass Dhanbahadur. In a moment this élite group was well ahead of the rest of the field which stretched back to the ridge.

Trevor came off the ridge onto the downhill section with

Hastabir, but moving slowly and cautiously, and the sight of the long drop was already tying his stomach into knots. 'You go on,' he shouted to Hastabir, 'I will only hold you up.'

But the Gurkha havildar made no move to leave him. And Trevor felt trapped in his own fear, his mind working desperately to find some way out because he knew he could never finish the race. He suddenly stumbled and collapsed against a large boulder. 'My ankle!' he cried out. 'I have twisted it.'

Hastabir's eyes were as angry as a tiger's, savage in his contempt at this feeble subterfuge. 'Coward!' he snarled out like a wild animal. '*Kaphar!* If Dillee were alive . . . .' He turned away and stepped out from behind the boulder, and then Trevor realized that Hastabir was going to make the long jump away from the line of footholds taken by the rest of the field.

'Not that way!' Trevor shouted.

'I have to make up the points you will lose,' Hastabir said coldly before turning and jumping in one movement.

Down among the spectators, Brigadier Peterson had focused his binoculars on the boulder. 'Good God!' he cried out at Hastabir's great leap. And then he saw Trevor hobble out from behind the boulder, fall to the ground, struggle to his feet again with obvious difficulty.

There was a petrified silence among the spectators for a moment, followed by a great gasp as Trevor sent his body hurtling into space behind Hastabir.

Hands held above his head, Trevor dropped into the void. Beneath him Hastabir had negotiated the jump and was bounding on to the next foothold. And then Trevor landed, and the pain shot through his leg into his body and he cried out. He spun, tried to keep his balance, fell sprawling along the ground scattering the sharp, loose stones in all directions, his bare arms and legs gashed and bleeding.

'Dillee!' he cried out. 'Dillee!' as he rolled over and over. And the last thing he saw was a giant boulder coming up to meet him.

The Bullet-Proof Head

The bullet which hit Rifleman Gorbir Gurung in the head should have killed him. It certainly would have killed anybody else.

The Afridi, hidden among the rocks on the hillside which walled the pass, had taken careful aim with all the skill of his race, knowing that his target was well within range. But Gorbir had just sat back on his heels, partly stunned for a moment, before shaking his close-cropped head to clear the mist which had formed in front of his eyes.

Later, when the regiment's doctor examined Gorbir's head, he was astonished to find a dent in the forehead, some broken skin and a bit of bruising, but that was all. As the doctor said in the Mess that night to an audience of officers who for once listened to him with attention. 'If it had not been for the evidence of my own eyes I just would not have believed it. Let me tell you, in my time I've seen a few wounds which would have proved fatal if it had not been for the sheer guts and physical strength of the Gurkha. But this chap today was saved by the almost iron-like structure of his cranium.'

Two people in the 15th Gurkha Rifle Regiment were not surprised. One was Gorbir Gurung himself, a man of the hills, quiet, simple. He loved the regiment; it was his whole world, a haven from the squalid, hard environment of his home village tucked away in a fold in back-of-beyond hills to the west of Kathmandu. He had been bullied as a boy, treated with callousness because of his simpleness, driven to do all the most physically difficult or unsavoury tasks. And he had been a source of amusement from time to time for the rougher youths of the village who pelted him with stones to see them bounce off his head. Then at last he had been old enough to slip away one night and walk for three weeks across the

82

mountains and the rickety contraptions which bridged the deep gullies, to the Recruiting Centre.

The 15th Gurkha Rifle Regiment, as the 15th Gurkha Rifles was called in those days, became his new parent. Although life was not a complete sinecure, the taunts about his simplicity lacked the vicious element of scorn that had marred his childhood, and the scrapes he somehow managed to get into were never very serious. He was not a perfect soldier, but he was loyal, honest and friendly.

The other person who was not surprised was the regiment's subedar-major, because as far as he was concerned Gorbir should never, in the first place, have been enrolled in the 15th. The young Gurkha was so dim-witted it was only natural that his head was rock-hard. But that having been said, Gorbir was still a member of the regiment, and as he had been wounded – the bullet might have only bounced off his head but he had nevertheless been wounded – he must be sent back to the Regimental Centre for convalescence.

Having come to this conclusion, the subedar-major promptly put his thoughts into action. The doctor considered objecting to the loss of a most interesting experimental subject, but did not feel sufficiently confident to run foul of the subedar-major.

So Gorbir found himself back at Dehra Dun in the foothills of the Himalayas, a green, cool and civilised place after the barren, hot and inhospitable Khyber Pass. And here he might have spent several months happily doing no more than light fatigues but for events stirring in the Lushai Hills 1,000 miles south-east of Dehra Dun, which were to have a considerable effect on his life.

The Lushai Hills run parallel to the Bay of Bengal, bordered by Cachar to the north, the Chittagong Hill Tract to the west and Burma to the south and east. Range upon range of mountains, mostly unexplored by the British until the late nineteenth century, extend for some 260 miles north to south, and 120 miles east to west. Rising to over 9,000 feet in places, the ranges are separated by deep valleys and cloaked in either dense jungle or evergreen oaks and sweet-scented alpine forests.

The rapid growth of tea-gardens throughout Southern Cachar in the 1860s alarmed the Lushais in much the same way as the encroachment of the settlers and buffalo hunters had roused the American Indians.

Towards the end of 1870, the chiefs of the most powerful Lushai tribes gathered for a meeting in the village of one of their number. Like the American Indians they sought a way to curb this danger to their hereditary hunting grounds in the Lushai Hills. In the council house they discussed the situation through several, long, frosty nights, finally reaching a unanimous decision to make almost simultaneous raids along a wide front, spreading such fear among the tea-planters and their coolies that the tea-gardens would be abandoned and any attempt to encroach deeper into the hills would be curtailed.

In January 1871, the war parties emerged from their mountain villages onto the plains and foothills of Assam. For the next two months they spread terror and destruction from Cachar to the Chittagong Hills Tract, burning tea-gardens and villages, looting, slaughtering coolies and villagers and taking many captives, including the six-year old daughter of a tea-garden manager.

When news of the raids reached Calcutta, the Viceroy was alarmed at their magnitude and ferocity, which exceeded all previous experience. He was determined to punish the Lushais, but the season was late and to involve troops in the hills during the rains was to court disaster. Accordingly, plans were made to launch a punitive expedition towards the end of the year.

Meanwhile, the tea-garden managers demanded protection against any further raids, at least for the next two months before the monsoon kept the Lushai warriors in their villages. To meet this request, it was decided to establish military posts on all the estates until the punitive expedition was launched. The 15th Gurkha Rifle Regiment, which had only recently arrived in the area after a momentous move across India from one frontier to another, was given the job. But the regiment was under strength because of leave and sickness, so reinforcements were called for from Dehra Dun. A draft was quickly assembled and despatched, and among its members was Gorbir Gurung.

To Gorbir the move was not entirely unwelcome. He had never been to India's North-East Frontier and, although the journey proved to be tedious, the tea-garden was a pleasant surprise. The neat ranks of dark green tea-bushes covered a hillside which had a breathtaking view to the distant mountains. The red roof of the manager's bungalow peeped out above an arbour of trees. The coolies' quarters bustled with the families of the tea-pickers, and the laughter of their friendly children gave Gorbir a feeling of warmth and contentment.

Gorbir was one of a party of eight Gurkhas detailed to guard the tea-garden, each man armed with the new breech-loading Snider-Enfield rifle. In charge was Havildar Manbahadur Gurung, the three stripes on his arm indicating a rank equivalent to a sergeant, and his bearing was an accurate pointer to a tough, experienced soldier.

Manbahadur was not very happy with the situation. He could not adequately protect an area of some two square miles with a squad of eight. But the battalion had to provide many such posts among the numerous tea-gardens, apart from its normal duties, and the colonel sahib had decided that the mere presence of the Gurkhas should be sufficient to deter at least the smaller bands of Lushai marauders.

On arrival at the garden, the havildar was met by one of the manager's assistants and guided to the small outpost erected by the garden coolies. Manbahadur could not fault the work. Behind an *abattis* of sharply pointed bamboo stakes which fringed the perimeter like so many porcupines, was a stoutly built block house with loopholes.

Manbahadur led his men through the gate and across the small compound between the fence and the block house. And when the assistant had left, the havildar had a good look around the fields of fire, and the accommodation. Each man was shown his firing position and where to keep his kit. Then Manbahadur made out a sentry duty roster.

Three days later, Captain Fuller rode over from his company headquarters. He was a good-looking man in his early thirties with a pencil moustache and piercing blue eyes in a very sunburnt face. His Hawkes patent cork helmet, covered with a white cloth, was at a slight angle on his head. He wore khaki uniform like his men, but with black, calf length boots. His revolver was in a buttoned holster at his belt.

Dismounting, he handed the reins to one of the men. 'Is all well, Manbahadur?'

'Yes, Sahib.'

'And the Lushais?'

'No reports, nor any sign of them, Sahib. There are not sufficient men to carry out a proper patrol. But I try to cover as much ground as possible twice a day.'

'I doubt if they will attempt a raid,' Fuller reassured him. 'But if you were attacked I think you should be able to hold out in the block house long enough for reinforcements to come to your aid.'

'That we will do, Sahib, never fear.'

Fuller then inspected the block house, approved of what he saw, and finally glanced over the other men in the squad. 'Ah, Manbahadur,' he exclaimed suddenly. 'I see you have a secret weapon to confront the enemy.'

The havildar looked surprised. Fuller placed a hand on Gorbir's shoulders. 'The man with the bullet-proof head,' he explained, smiling to show that he was not being sarcastic.

Manbahadur grinned broadly, the other Gurkhas chuckled, and Gorbir smiled shyly.

The sound of an approaching horse made Fuller remove his hand and look towards the perimeter gate. Presently horse and rider came into view. The rider was an overweight man in his late forties, with a very red face but kindly eyes and a friendly smile. He reined in and saluted with his riding crop.

'A very good afternoon, sir,' he greeted Fuller. 'Jack Gilling is the name. Manager of this tea-garden.'

Fuller returned the greeting with a nod, showing the reserved side of his nature until such time as he could gauge Gilling more closely.

'I was wondering, sir,' Gilling continued, 'if you would care to join me in some refreshment.' Adding quickly as though he had seen some indication of refusal cloud Fuller's face, 'Don't get much chance to entertain visitors out here in the blue. One of the drawbacks of this type of work.'

'I should be delighted, sir,' Fuller said and, after a few words of instruction to Manbahadur, mounted his horse and accompanied Gilling to the manager's bungalow.

Within a short time Fuller was glad he had accepted the

invitation. Gilling proved to be an excellent host and amusing company, and he lived very comfortably. With the wine and conversation, darkness came quickly and quietly and unseen by the two men on the verandah until servants came out with hurricane-lamps to hang on the hooks suspended from the beams.

'I had not realized it was so late,' said Fuller. 'It's a fair ride back to my HQ, and my second-in-command is inclined to be nervous. He may well have sent out a search party already. As it is he was most disturbed to think that I was riding here, unescorted, and perhaps he was right, but there are few times when I can enjoy the solace of a long ride.'

'Why not stay for dinner, and I can put you up for the night,' said Gilling, adding, on seeing Fuller was half-tempted, 'Don't worry about your lieutenant. Write him a note and I'll send a runner to deliver it within the hour. My men can outrun a horse in this terrain by making use of the many short-cuts.'

'Very well, Jack,' agreed Fuller, and wrote a short note.

While Fuller and Gilling were dining, from a nearby, jungle-capped hill the Lushai chief, Cherlalla, watched the pin-points of light from the hurricane-lamps. He was of medium height, sturdily built and he had Mongolian features. His hair was worn long, parted in the middle, plastered flat across the crown, the braided tresses drawn into a knot at the back of his head.

Behind him, down the reverse slope of the hill, waited his war party of more than fifty. Like him, each warrior wore a single cloth wrapped round the waist. Over one shoulder was slung a haversack, protected by a bear or tiger skin guard, the fighting dao in its bamboo sheath over the other, and musket to hand.

Cherlalla continued to watch until the hurricane-lamps were extinguished. Then he rose to his feet, and moved down the hill towards the tea-garden, his warriors following. He led the way with certainty in the darkness because he had already reconnoitred the route, and knew when to change direction and make a wide sweep to the north to avoid the Gurkha post, and then come in through the jungle to attack his first objective, the coolie lines.

There was a tinge of dawn in the sky as the war party slipped stealthily through the belt of jungle to the north of the tea-garden, and up to its fringe with the wide clearing which had been cut out to make room for the coolie lines. Here Cherlalla intended to wait until there was more light before he launched his savage men at the lines where the innocent tea-garden coolies and their children lay asleep. But suddenly a dark figure rose out of the ground at his feet and screamed, a long, piercing scream directly into his face, causing him to step back and almost stumble. The woman who had left her hut to relieve herself at the jungle's edge screamed again before a Lushai warrior cut her down angrily with his *dao*.

But the first scream had brought Fuller out of a deep sleep with a start. For a moment he lay on the bed wondering if he had really heard it; then the woman screamed again. He swung his legs out of the bed as muskets barked in the distant coolie lines, and the fearful war cries broke the quiet, mingling harshly with the wailing of the coolies and their families as they awoke and became aware of the terror which had torn its way into the garden.

Fuller pulled on his trousers over his long underwear, pushed his feet into the boots, seized his gun belt and began buckling it on as he rushed from the room onto the verandah. He was just in time to see Gilling running from the bungalow towards the coolie lines, double-barrelled gun in hand.

'Jack!' Fuller shouted. 'Come back, you fool.'

But Gilling did not break his stride as he ran towards the lines which were now a blazing inferno. Many figures fled screaming, human torches in the darkness, others ran wildly, chased by the Lushais who were howling with savage glee as their *daos* swung red in the firelight.

Then Gilling was among them. A group of Lushais rushed to meet him. He fired both barrels, there were crumpled forms on the ground, then he disappeared beneath a crowd of warriors. Fuller hurried down the bungalow steps and round to the back where his horse had been stabled. There was no sign as yet of the Lushais, or of the servants who must have fled while they had the chance.

As he led his horse out of the stable, he could hear the

howling of approaching Lushais. He swung himself up onto the unsaddled horse and kicked his boots into its sides. The horse, already restless from the noise, needed little bidding. It raced along the dirt track between the arbour of trees towards the Gurkha outpost.

Fuller hung on grimly. In the ever-increasing light of daybreak he could see the block house above the *abattis* just ahead. Then a musket was discharged, the slug missing the horse's head and whistling past over Fuller's shoulder. The horse reared with a cry. Fuller felt himself slipping and then he was on the ground. The horse rolled onto its back its hind legs just missing his head, then it struggled onto its feet, eyes mad with terror, and galloped out of sight.

Fuller was reaching frantically for his revolver when a Snider was fired, and then another. And then Manbahadur was at his side. 'Hurry, Sahib!' They ran the last few yards to the open gate and through it. The gate was pushed shut, the door of the block house beckoned, and Fuller was bustled through it, and heard it boom shut behind him. A moment later there was a rattling along the outer walls of the block house as the Lushais fired a volley. They were answered by the Gurkhas at the loopholes.

'You are not hurt, Sahib?'

'No. But Gilling Sahib is dead and the coolie lines ablaze, and many innocent people slaughtered by these savages.'

'The bungalow is alight too,' said Gorbir from his vantage point at a loophole.

Fuller nodded his head. 'We will have to hold out here for some hours, I think, Havildar. But help will come. Gilling Sahib had two runners permanently placed outside the estate to run to Company HQ in the event of an attack.'

But one of the runners had already lost his head to a Lushai *dao*. The other, sorely wounded, had managed to escape, but was making slow, painful progress towards the Gurkha headquarters some ten miles distant.

For the next three hours the small band held out against the screaming horde. Inside the block house the noise was ear-splitting as the Sniders fired out their resistance, and the smell of cordite hung in the smoky air. Two of the Gurkhas were dead, a third lay mortally wounded in a corner. From his loophole, Gorbir kept watch for any movement in the full daylight which had come. A few musket shots had passed close by him, but his bullet-proof head had not as yet been put to the test again. And it seemed to him that for every Lushai killed another took his place, but he continued mechanically, loading a fresh cartridge in the breech, taking careful aim when a target presented itself, firing then tilting the Snider over to allow the spent cartridge to be eased out of the breech.

There seemed to be extensive activity near the gate of sharpened bamboo stakes, and he called Manbahadur's attention to this. Almost at once there was an onslaught of musket volleys, and another Gurkha gave a moan and fell from the loopholed gallery to the floor of the block house. Gorbir and Manbahadur began firing as rapidly as possible at the Lushais swarming around the gate, and were joined by Fuller who had armed himself with a rifle from one of the dead soldiers.

The gate suddenly swung open and a group of warriors ran towards the door. Although several were shot dead, two managed to reach the door, leaving a wooden barrel before escaping through the gate.

'What is it?' Fuller cried out.

'Gunpowder. Stand away from the door!'

But at that moment Cherlalla fired his musket, the gunpowder ignited and the door blew open with a great roar. Fuller was hurled across the room, his whole body filled with pain as he hit the far wall. There was a blackness pierced by red flashes, a hollowness which echoed with screams and war cries, and then silence.

From somewhere far away he felt himself travelling back to reality. His ears were being pulled to bring him back to consciousness, and now he could hear Manbahadur's voice urging him on. He opened his eyes, and the havildar was looking down at him.

'What happened?' Fuller asked before memory came rushing back as well, and he sat up abruptly and groaned.

'Steady, Sahib,' whispered Manbahadur. 'Be very careful when you look around.'

Almost knowing what he would see, Fuller turned his eyes away from the havildar and looked at the crowd of curious Lushais staring at him with a certain wonder, fascinated by his fair hair and blue eyes.

Fuller tried to speak, then croaked, 'How many of us?'

'You and me, and Gorbir and Dhanbahadur. The others are dead, as we should have been. We should have fought to the last,' he said bitterly, 'but the explosion knocked all of us out, and killed two more men.'

'There is no shame in being captured,' Fuller tried to console him. 'And never fear, the battalion will not be long in coming to our aid.'

There was a stir among the tribesmen, and Cherlalla stepped out to look down at Fuller. Their eyes met for a moment, then the chief gave a grunt and turned abruptly on his heels, shouting out commands.

A little Indian boy from the coolie lines said to Fuller, 'We are leaving for their village now. Quick, Sahib, you must stand up. Anyone who cannot keep up or falls by the wayside is killed at once.'

Manbahadur and Gorbir helped Fuller to his feet. He swayed for a moment, and they were reluctant to release their hold of him, but he insisted that he would be all right.

The long line moved out along the path that led to the higher hills. There was no semblance of order. The warriors walked in groups or singly, and chattered incessantly. But all the time keeping an eye on their prisoners – those wilting, terrified coolies, women and children whose lives had been spared to become slaves in the Lushai village.

'What is your name?' Fuller asked the Indian boy.

'I am called Chico. All my family were slain this morning, Sahib,' he added, but without any outward sign of emotion.

'You seem to know the ways of these savages.'

'Some people escaped from them once, and they told their story to the elders, and I listened.'

'How far is the village?'

'About two days journey at the speed they travel. They will only stop briefly tonight for food. We must keep up with them, Sahib, I promise you it is most important.'

Fuller nodded, wondering how much of the boy's story was true, but he looked bright enough and had obviously decided to attach himself to the Gurkha group. He could well prove useful as he seemed to have some knowledge of the Lushai language.

The Lushai column set off at a steady pace, stopping only twice in the next four hours to allow warriors and captives to relieve themselves. The heat of the day gathered about them like the glass walls of a greenhouse, but with the door open to let in the swirling clouds of dust stirred up by the hundreds of feet.

Fuller's own feet began to ache and burn for his half-length boots had not been made for a long march and his body was still painful from the pummelling it had received in the explosion. He tried to hide his anguish, knowing that he had to set his men an example. And he also knew he had to keep going, because Chico had been right.

Every now and then he would see a body at the roadside – some old man or woman who had collapsed and had been promptly despatched, or the pitiful sight of a young child's corpse. He thought the day would never end.

The column moved on relentlessly along rough goat paths that criss-crossed the hills through a jungle of tall trees and tangled undergrowth, all brown and dry and seemingly ready to burst into flames from one hot ray of sunshine.

Little Chico was a tower of strength, indefatigable, bright eyes seemingly unaffected by the conditions. At one time, when Fuller thought he could not move another step, and the three Gurkhas, even the tough Manbahadur, were wilting, the Indian boy produced a water bottle. There was enough for each of them to have a mouthful of water, to swirl it around dry lips, trying to make it last for an eternity, before taking the final swallow.

Towards evening they began to climb more steeply, and there was a coolness in the air, and patches of green grass and green leaves, until the forest was all green, with splashes of colour from rhododendrons and wild flowers. Then they came out of the forest and the Lushai Hills lay ahead, range after range, rising in tiers, the distant ranges several steps higher, here and there great scars where the Lushais had cleared the *jooms*, or fields, for cultivation. Their method of agriculture was to burn stretches of forest, plant the year's crop in the clearing then move off to another patch the following season.

To the south further ranges blurred in the haze of the far-off horizon. In the valley below a river emerged in stretches of silver from a canopy of thick jungle.

The column halted for an evening meal of corn. 'Will we stay here the night?' Fuller asked Chico.

'No, Sahib. I think we will walk all night.'

Fuller groaned inwardly. His feet had eventually gone so numb that he had been able to hobble without too much difficulty, but now pain indicated returning circulation. By the time he moved out again, his feet would be instruments of torture. He did not think he would have much chance of escaping in the darkness, although the others might.

But any thoughts of escape were soon dashed, because after the meal Cherlalla came up to see them, gave some orders, then departed. At once a group of warriors descended on their Gurkha prisoners and tied their hands in front of them. Then a rope was passed through so that the four men were linked together.

There was a great deal of shouting further along the ridge, and the column moved out into the night. A Lushai led Fuller and the Gurkhas like pack animals along a track which was only just discernible, and seemed to follow every fold in the ground. If one man fell, the others would stumble over him. The Lushais screamed, and pushed them upright, and pulled at the ropes.

The rest of the night was a jumbled nightmare of climbing, scrambling downhill, a straight run, then the whole pattern repeated. Fuller's wrists burned from the thongs which bit into the flesh, and his body ached from the bruises of many falls, and his feet felt as though they were no longer a part of him.

Then at last it was daybreak, and they came abruptly out of the bamboo and onto the banks of a river. Here there was a long halt; their hands were freed, and they were able to have some semblance of a wash.

'The village is only a few hours away, now,' Chico said.

'After what we have been through,' Manbahadur said gruffly, 'the going can only be better.'

'What will happen to us at the village?' asked the other rifleman, Dhanbahadur, who had a nasty cut across his cheek where he had fallen into a tangle of undergrowth during the night.

Fuller summoned up a reserve of strength and optimism. 'I

93

feel sure we will be kept as hostages, or something of that nature,' he tried to reassure the others. 'In any case, the battalion cannot be far behind. The Colonel Sahib will have had trackers out long before now.'

It is what I would have done, Fuller thought. But he was not too sure about the colonel, who might be swayed by political arguments to leave the Lushais alone until the punitive expedition was launched later in the year. He shook the thought from his mind. 'Yes, the Colonel Sahib will have us free in no time.'

'We are about to move out,' Chico said just then. 'And I do not think they will tie your hands again.'

As the column moved along the river bank, the Lushai guards made no attempt to retie their prisoners. They crossed the river along a weir made of bamboo and stone for catching fish. On the far side a path led through thick jungle which seemed to grow outwards because of the steepness of the gradient. For 1,000 feet or so the column had to move in single file. Then abruptly the path came out of the jungle and straightened across a *joom*. The Lushais began to chatter excitedly, and wave their arms and muskets in the air. Fuller guessed their village was close. And presently they crossed another *joom*, and there was Cherlalla's village, near the top of the ridge, a little way down the slope as a protection against high winds.

There was a loopholed stockade, excellently constructed on the most approved principle, Fuller noted with his military mind. The entrance to the village was through a passage of strong timber defended by a solid gate. Beyond the stockade, the streets radiated in all directions following spurs or slopes. The houses, about eighteen feet long by twelve feet wide, were all gable-ended and constructed of a strong timber framework with walls and floors of bamboo matting and the roof thatched with grass. There was a large verandah at the front.

In a moment the village streets were alive with people of all ages, screaming with delight as they ran out of the gate to welcome the return of their triumphant warriors. Fuller and the Gurkhas were the main attraction, and the warriors detailed as their guards had to beat off the many curious villagers. But a group of young Lushais managed to crowd round Fuller, astonished at his fair skin. They asked him by signs to turn up the sleeves of his tunic. There were loud cries of amazed delight at finding that the skin above the wrists was even whiter than the hands, which to British eyes seemed very sun-tanned. Even then some of the more sceptical were not convinced that the white would not come off until they had rubbed the skin well with wet fingers, examining their fingers carefully after the process.

Eventually, the Lushai guards managed to gain control, and hustle the prisoners into what seemed to be an unused storeroom. The door was closed quickly, and heavy wooden bolts were heard to draw shut outside. For the first time the four of them were alone.

There were no windows in the room, but some light came from high up where there appeared to be narrow slits. The floor was of timber, as were the walls which Manbahadur tapped, and reported that they were very tough.

The room was quite bare. There was no earthenware vessel containing water, and certainly nothing for the calls of nature.

'I suppose somebody will be along presently,' the havildar said.

Fuller nodded his head. For the moment he was content to sit on the floor, his back propped against the wall, his feet stretched out. 'We might as well rest while we can,' he suggested. 'Then we can make plans later.'

'Perhaps they will allow Chico to come and see us. He is sure to have information.'

Fuller made no comment. But Gorbir came up to him. 'Sahib, I think you must take off your boots.' He knelt at his officer's feet.

'If I take them off,' Fuller said, 'I doubt if I will ever be able to put them on again.'

'But you could not get far with them on,' Manbahadur pointed out.

'Oh, very well.' Gorbir tried to ease the boots off. Fuller winced. 'I think they have become part of my leg.'

Gorbir glanced at the havildar. 'If only we had something to cut the boots.'

At this, Dhanbahadur quietly slipped out a small knife. 'They did not know I had this on me,' he explained.

'Oh *shabash*, well done, Dhanbahadur.'

The havildar cut down the side of one boot and Gorbir eased it off. Both men could hardly suppress an exclamation of surprise. Quickly Manbahadur cut the other boot, and when this had been removed they looked at the feet anxiously.

'Not a very attractive sight,' said Fuller in English.

'Huzoor?' the havildar queried.

'I am sure they look worse than they feel,' Fuller reverted to Gurkhali.

Gorbir shook his head as he felt the feet tenderly. They were cut and almost blue, and covered with suppurating blisters. Manbahadur said, 'If we are to escape, Sahib, something must be done for these.' He turned to the others. 'Make a great deal of noise on that door until someone comes.'

The two Gurkhas beat on the door and kicked it with their boots, and shouted until at last the bolts were shot back and the door opened. Two Lushais, highly suspicious, with muskets at the ready, covered the room. Manbahadur touched Fuller's feet to indicate that medical treatment was necessary. The Lushai guard commander gave a grunt, then slammed the door shut and crashed the bolts home.

'Do not worry,' Fuller said, seeing the distress on his men's faces, although he knew they would still do so. However, they did not have long to worry, because quite soon the bolts were drawn again and this time Chico came in with a *chatti* of water and a bundle under his arms, followed by a Lushai with bowls of food. Placing the bowls on the floor, the Lushai again shut the door behind him.

'Ah, Chico, we are very glad to see you,' Fuller said.

'I told them I was your slave, Sahib,' the Indian boy said with a chuckle. 'Now then, let us have a look at your feet,' he added in a different voice, no doubt imitating the doctor who used to visit the tea-garden. 'We will soon have you up and about,' he chirped in English, then squatted near Fuller and opened the bundle. 'There is nothing like bear's fat, Sahib.' And after he had washed the feet and dried them, he applied the fat generously. Fuller would have sworn that he could feel the pain leaving immediately.

'Let it stay like that for a few hours, Sahib.'

'Thank you, Dr Chico. Now tell us what is happening

outside.'

'A lot of excitement over their attack on the tea-garden, Sahib. But nothing definite has been decided about you and your men. From what I could overhear and understand, it would seem that they believe they can exchange you for a number of the new rifles. Meanwhile, they will take a rest after their adventure. Tomorrow night a big celebration is planned, with feasting and drinking and dancing. It will be a long, noisy night, Sahib.'

'Just the sort of conditions for us to attempt an escape,' Fuller said. 'If we can get out of here, it looks very solid. What is there on these sides and to the back of us?'

'There are houses on either side, but to the back there is open ground for a short distance to the stockade.'

'That would be the way out, if we had some tool to cut through this timber. Otherwise, there is only the door, and so far the sentries have been very alert.'

'They are afraid of what Cherlalla will do to them if they let you escape,' Chico explained.

'Well, we will just have to work out some plan. You had better stay on the outside, Chico, where you will be more useful to us. See what you can find out, but on no account are you to take unnecessary risks.'

'I am too smart,' the Indian boy said cheekily. Then banged on the door to be let out.

The rest of the day passed slowly for the captives. They were allowed out singly to relieve themselves. Chico came twice with food, but had no optimistic news. He had, however, worked miracles on Fuller's feet which were much less swollen and the blisters looked drier. The following morning Chico produced a pair of sandals which fitted reasonably comfortably after the feet had been carefully bound in cloth.

At midday when Chico returned with food and water he seemed quite elated. 'There are two new sentries. And they are annoyed because they wanted to enjoy the celebration tonight.'

'And how does that help us?'

'Well, Sahib, I would be very surprised if they do not slip off to the celebration all the same. Once bolted in for the night, they think you will be quite safe. They know I cannot open the door because the bolts are too high and too tight for my little strength. So after the evening meal they will be keen to get away.'

'So they might become careless if we can delay their departure,' Fuller said.

'We must entice one of them to come in with Chico,' Manbahadur suggested. 'We have Dhanbahadur's knife.'

'Yes, but there is one thing that worries me,' Fuller said. 'Why are we not on show at the celebration?'

'I had thought of that, Sahib,' Chico looked pleased with himself. 'It seems that Cherlalla has invited some chiefs from other villages, including one, a half-brother, who is jealous and not to be trusted. Cherlalla would dearly like to show you off to spite him, but he is afraid that this half-brother might try to steal you away in the confusion of the drunkenness and noise – or perhaps even do you some harm through envy.'

'Let us hope you are right, Chico.'

They worked out their plan of action, then Fuller asked Chico. 'Will you be coming with us?'

'Of course, Sahib.' He collected the empty dishes. 'Never fear. Chico will not let you down.'

The door opened to him. He turned towards Fuller, grinned cheekily, and was gone. And when the door had closed behind him, the others settled down to wait.

The room grew gloomy and then dark. From outside they caught faint sounds of shouting and laughing, sounds which grew louder and more concentrated until they merged with the sudden throb of drums, and the room flickered with firelight flashing through the slits under the roof.

The door burst open violently, and there were angry voices as Chico stumbled with the dishes. 'Why are you so late?' the first Lushai sentry demanded.

'I am only small,' Chico pleaded. 'And there are many dishes to carry, and the water.' He let the tears course down his little face.

'Oh give him a hand,' the other sentry said, 'or we will be here all night.'

'Stupid little fool,' the first Lushai muttered, pushing Chico in front of him, and following with the jug of water. And as he bent down to place the jug on the floor, he found the sharp point of a knife pressed against his throat.

'Do not move,' Chico said in Lushai. A little prod with the knife by Dhanbahadur convinced the man.

'You are taking a long time,' the second sentry called out.

'Tell him one of the prisoners looks very ill,' Chico said, as Manbahadur slid the man's *dao* from its sheath and moved to the side of the doorway. The second Lushai came bursting in, swearing, and the next moment Manbahadur had placed the razor sharp edge of the *dao* against his neck.

They tied up the two Lushais with the shoulder straps cut from the *dao* sheaths, and gagged them with strips torn from the waistcloth of one of the men.

Coming out into the open, Fuller was struck by the noise. It sounded as if every drum in Lushai Land was being beaten furiously, accompanied by the shouting, screaming voices of the inhabitants. Even if the sentries managed to get loose from their bonds, no one would hear their shouts for help.

Manbahadur bolted the door, then Chico led the way behind the houses and along a narrow path which skirted the stockade. The firelight made the night as bright as moonlight, and it was a wonder that nobody noticed them. But all attention was inwards towards the centre of the village where the revelry was at its most boisterous.

Chico brought them to a sudden halt. He whispered, 'The gateway is just past the next house. There are usually two sentries, one on each side.'

'Stay here,' Manbahadur said. Then he and Dhanbahadur, armed with the *daos*, moved quietly ahead and around the house. The firelight did not quite reach the gate and the first sentry was partly in shadow, looking down the main street towards the festival, his musket propped against the gate post. There was no sign of the other sentry.

Manbahadur darted across to the stockade wall and flattened himself against it. The sentry did not stir. Manbahadur edged his way closer. This one was as easy as taking a recruit on a military exercise, he thought as he brought down the *dao*. The sentry lurched forward without a sound, and the havildar caught him and eased his body back against the wall.

Dhanbahadur came up quickly to join the havildar. 'I cannot see another sentry.'

'They must have decided to dispense with him on this night of festivities,' Manbahadur suggested. 'Get the others.'

Meanwhile, he lifted the bar with trepidation. There was no cry of alarm. Slowly he edged open the gate, just enough for the others to slip through. He followed, easing the bar down through the gap, so when he shut the gate behind him, it fell into place.

Chico had been allowed out with a firewood collecting party, and had taken the opportunity to study the land. 'If we cross this *joom,* there is an old track I found going down through the jungle. The Lushais will be feasting all night so we should have a good start.'

Fuller put a hand on the little Indian boy's shoulder. 'Well done, Chico. Now show us the way.'

But they had only covered half the distance across the *joom* when the drumming and the noise stopped abruptly, followed almost at once by loud shouts. Cherlalla, taunted by his half-brother to prove that he really had Gurkha prisoners, and a British officer, had stormed off to the storehouse. In his drunken rage he had chopped down the bound and gagged sentries. Now, waving the blood-stained *dao* above his head, he raced for the gate followed by a howling mob. The gate was pulled open and they burst out into the night and across the *joom.*

'Run!' Chico screamed. 'We must reach the jungle.'

The tufted ground of the *joom* made running difficult, and Fuller's sandals were not suitable for running. He carried them in his hand, but the rough ground bit into his bandaged feet. He struggled on, Gorbir by his side, encouraging him. Muskets began to rattle, a ragged volley, the slugs whistling wildly through the air.

Manbahadur and Dhanbahadur came back to help Fuller. 'Go on,' the officer shouted. 'Leave me!' His pleas were ignored.

'They are gaining,' Gorbir shouted, looking back. And the next thing he knew a musket slug had struck him on the head. He felt a sharp, burning blow across the side of his head as the slug was diverted and ricocheted into the night, and he heard a strike against flesh and a low moan as the bullet found another target. Then he was kneeling on the ground, dizzy, blood trickling into his mouth.

Now Gorbir could hear shouts and shots, but the shouts were in Gurkhali, and the shots were a steady volley by trained soldiers firing Sniders. He could just see the fighting patrol from the battalion rushing towards him. Then they were past and in amongst the Lushais who turned and fled.

Manbahadur and Dhanbahadur served with the 15th Gurkha Rifle Regiment for many more years, rising to high rank. Chico was educated by a grateful regiment, and became an outstanding doctor.

As for Gorbir? Well, he remained, simple, loyal, friendly, but still finding himself in many scrapes. And when he was in trouble the usual thing was to remind him, 'If it were not for your bullet-proof head, Fuller Sahib would still be alive today.'

Short, Back And All Over

When Lieutenant Woolley, in the last year of World War II, bought a crate of cut-price hair cream for the Gurkhas' Canteen Shop, he believed that his purchase was a splendid example of initiative.

Captain Brown, the battalion quartermaster, who had risen from the ranks of a British regiment, was always muttering about the inadequacies of junior Emergency Commission Officers, and of his assistant in particular. Woolley felt that at last he would draw praise from the crusty old ranker.

But the look on Brown's face when he was told sent a shiver down Woolley's spine. Spots of white foam at the corner of the quartermaster's mouth as he spluttered to find words only confirmed Woolley's sudden foreboding.

'Here,' the quartermaster managed to speak at last, catching hold of his Gurkha clerk by the arm and leading him up to Woolley. 'Take a look at his head. His head, Woolley. Take a look, you blithering young idiot.'

Woolley looked at the shaven head and felt his stomach turn over. At that time the men of the Gurkha Brigade were still required under an ancient military directive to keep their heads shaven. In his anxiety to impress the quartermaster, Woolley had completely forgotten this vital fact.

When the word reached the Officers' Mess, the roar of derision was heard a long way off. Poor Woolley found himself in that unenviable position of being held up as a dreadful example to others. The crate of hair cream stood unopened, collecting dust in a back room, a constant reminder to new officers of *Woolley's Blunder*.

It was little wonder that whenever Woolley saw a shaven Gurkha head he sent up a little prayer that in some way the hair would grow overnight, or that the old act would be repealed.

And he was not the only one who had this dream.

'Get your hair cut!' had long been the prerogative of the British regiments. In the Gurkha regiments this privilege was long denied, because how could you possibly order soldiers to have their hair cut when they were all as shorn as convicts?

Admittedly, Subedar-Major Bhimlal Thapa of the 15th was able to derive some pleasure from the shaven heads of his troops. He would trot along the ranks on his short, thick legs, eyes narrowed, Mongolian features hard and ruthless. Suddenly he would pounce on a shaking little rifleman and whip off his Gurkha hat, exposing a wide expanse of shaven head, except for one lock of hair, the *tupi,* which had to remain because without it the Gurkha could not be pulled up to Heaven.

Rubbing the palm of his hand over the billiard ball surface, Bhimlal would growl angrily and thrust his hand under the rifleman's nose.

'Look at that . . .Almost cut to ribbons by the bristles. GET YOUR HEAD SHAVED!'

The rifleman was whisked away immediately to the regimental barber's shop which consisted of a stool at the back of the washhouse, where the barber applied a thick lather to his customer's head, then wielded a cut-throat razor to remove the offending fluff.

This unhappy state of affairs lasted for a long time. Meanwhile, the subedar-majors would often hide behind trees to watch with envy as NCOs inspected squads of British troops. How sweet was the explosive roar that echoed around the parade ground: 'Am I hurting you? I must be because I am standing on your hair. GET YOUR HAIR CUT!'

Those magical words were like a glass of neat rum to Bhimlal's system, sending sheets of flame coursing through his veins. And the afterwards was like the hangover from too much rum as, sad and dejected, he would return to his own barracks.

But a change was on the way, although what originally brought it about is hard to say. Perhaps a photograph in some magazine left lying around in a rash moment by a British officer – who should have known better – of a dashing male film star with well-groomed hair, might have stirred a hidden craving. Whatever the reason, towards the end of World War II a request was made to repeal the ancient military act which required Gurkha soldiers to keep their heads shaven.

In hundreds of officers' messes, and in boarding houses where retired army officers remembered the good old days, the news had a shattering effect. Major Bryne-Nuttall was heard to refuse a double Scotch; Colonel Pierponte-Chumlee went off the end of the pier at Brighton in his bath-chair. But eventually permission was given for hair growing to start.

The whole characteristic of the Gurkha Brigade began to change. Gurkhas could now be found in all sorts of nooks and crannies, secretly examining their heads with pocket mirrors to estimate the rate of growth. One or two of the sharper ones even organised a sweepstake, although this ended in uproar when it was discovered that one of the more artful riflemen was using a hair restorer.

To the regimental barbers it meant a completely new way of life. Cut-throat razors were replaced by clippers, scissors and combs. One barber, more go-ahead than his colleagues, ordered some electric clippers; but he was confused over voltages and the other barbers were rather glad they had not followed his example.

But the person most overjoyed by the new order was undoubtedly Lieutenant Woolley. At that time there was a shortage of hair cream in the district. But Woolley's crate was now brought out from the back room and dusted down.

Within the course of the day its complete contents had been sold, much to the chagrin of the other Gurkha regiments who had been unable to buy sufficient stock for their own men.

In the Officers' Mess of the 15th Gurkha Rifles, the roar that went up this time was a cheer for 'Good old Woolley.' And even Captain Brown managed to mutter: 'Well done, son.' But he could not help adding under his breath, 'Of all the jammy sods.'

Meanwhile the subedar-majors watched and waited as the hair sprouted, first like bristles on a clothes brush, and then softening into long, black locks and thickening down to the shirt collars. At last the day came when the subedar-majors no longer had to watch British troops from behind cover, and suffer chronic indigestion and various nervous disorders.

They could now march proudly onto their own parade grounds and thunder majestically, 'GET YOUR HAIR CUT!'

Loyal To Their Salt

As a Gurkha he would never have surrendered willingly, choosing rather to rush some enemy machine-gun and die like a warrior. But it had been the General Sahib's order: an unconditional surrender on 15 February 1942, of all forces under his command in Singapore and the Malay Peninsula.

Subedar Lalbahadur Gurung of the 2/15th Gurkha Rifles felt the shame greatly. But on reflection realized that the war was not really over for him. In the Japanese prison camp he would still have to fight, but his weapons would be patience, tact and cunning. The British officers had been removed to another camp, and the subedar-major had been killed at Seremban, so the care of the men became his responsibility as the senior Gurkha officer. He expected staunch help from the junior Gurkha officers and NCOs to maintain discipline, prevent depression and to keep an eye on everyone's general health.

During the first days of captivity, the Japanese treated the Gurkha POWs reasonably well, but Lalbahadur was suspicious because the enemy's behaviour in the field seemed to indicate that a tough, ruthless attitude would have been adopted. All was made clear when Captain Watanabe, the camp commandant, invited the subedar to his bungalow. It had belonged to some rich *tuan,* and was conveniently sited to become the captain's headquarters.

'Sit down, sit down,' Watanabe said, pointing to an easy chair. He spoke in Urdu, the *lingua franca* between the two men.

Presently an Indian servant came in with tea, placing Lalbahadur in a delicate situation. The idea of taking tea with a Jap was repugnant when he thought of what the enemy had done to his colonel sahib. But to refuse at this stage would show open hostility and undermine his chances of ensuring good treatment for his men. He decided that he had to accept the refreshment. The colonel sahib would surely have understood.

It was while they drank tea that Watanabe revealed the reason behind the obvious ploy. 'For years you have been under the heel of the British Imperialists,' he said. 'Your country has been drained of its wealth for their benefit. Now you are free of the chains. Now you can get retribution. You and your men should join the Indian National Army. Thousands of Indian prisoners have already done so under the inspired leadership of Mohan Singh.'

Mohan Singh was an Indian Army captain who had been taken prisoner early in the campaign. As for the thousands of Indian Army prisoners – with their officers deliberately segregated, stunned by the collapse of their regimental world and, it seemed, the British Empire, the doubtful helped by physical coercion – more than 30,000 had defected to the INA.

Lalbahadur replied carefully. 'The honourable captain has unfortunately been misinformed, because the Gurkhas are not under the British yoke, and have no connection with India's desire to win Independence. We contracted our service to the British Raj, and indeed have done so for more than a hundred years, freely of our own choice, but swearing loyalty. As a Japanese officer you obviously respect the importance of honour, so you cannot expect us to betray ours.'

The Japanese captain's face remained impassive. 'I understand your beliefs, but I think you will find them misguided after a short stay in the camp. We will talk again.'

Lalbahadur got to his feet, and suddenly Watanabe slapped him across the face. It needed all Lalbahadur's self-control not to seize Watanabe by the throat. He drew himself up to attention, then turned towards the door. A burly Jap guard swung a vicious punch. The room spun with red, fiery stars, there was blood in his mouth and perhaps a broken tooth.

Heavy hands hurled him to the floor and he was kicked viciously in the side. He was violently sick, spewing over the expensive rugs the captain had planned to take back to Japan as booty. Watanabe screamed with rage, 'Get him out of here!' He was dragged to the door and across the verandah, then bounced down the steps and left sprawling in the dust.

Some of Lalbahadur's men came running bravely up to the bungalow, and were allowed to carry him back to the huts. Although the side of his face was already swelling, thankfully his teeth were intact. But his body ached with every movement.

'They have no right to treat you like this,' Jemadar Deobahadur protested. He was a young, newly promoted Gurkha officer.

'That was exactly what I told him,' the subedar spoke with some difficulty. 'He was not pleased.'

There were shouts outside and two Japanese guards rushed in, pushing the Gurkhas aside, seizing Lalbahadur. Their sadistic NCO followed, shouting, 'Outside. No stay in hut. Bad prisoner.' The subedar was hauled out into the sun and left sitting with his back against the hut.

Lalbahadur's jaw ached, and he closed his eyes as though this would bring him some relief. Was it all worth it? he asked himself. Then answered angrily, ashamed of the momentary doubt, of course! Yes, life had been good in the regiment. The relationship between British officer and rifleman was a mutual respect and genuine affection, and all through his service that had been the hallmark of the Gurkha regiment. The Gurkhas had always been loyal to their salt.

He had joined during World War I, and served in Mesopotamia. The heat outside the hut was nothing compared to the 120 degrees in the shade, if you could find any in the mile upon mile of desert where they had fought the Turks, and the smallpox, dysentery and plagues of flies. He was soon to learn that a Jap POW camp had its own virulent share of diseases.

The British officers had set a fine example. He remembered Steven Sahib at the Shumran Bend, sliced by the machine-gun he had charged, his sacrifice allowing C Company to overrun the Turk position, kukris and grenades taking a great toll and the trenches filled with enemy dead. And there was Jones Sahib, Binney Sahib, and so many others, then and later in times of peace, who had made the regiment a formation to be proud to belong to; and the Attestation Parade, when recruits

108

declared their loyalty to the British Sovereign – surely something to honour and uphold.

Yes, Binney Sahib who had held the road bridge against the Japs on the retreat to Slim, knocking out one enemy tank with an anti-tank rifle before a mortar bomb left his mangled body sprawled across the gun. It had been a desperate retreat all the way down the Malay Peninsula, fighting hard, not knowing if the situation had altered hour to hour; and on the next leg of withdrawal running into Jap road-blocks put up quickly by enemy infiltrators. Several times the battalion had been split, groups carrying on the fighting retreat, losing more men, meeting up again, continuing through dense jungle, marshes and rubber estates, many a brave deed going unnoticed.

And the moment he knew he would never forget, when they came upon Battalion HQ and found it had been overrun by the enemy. The dead were everywhere, including quite a few Japs. But tied to trees were the colonel sahib, the adjutant and two Gurkhas. They had been used as bayonet and sword targets while still alive. The colonel sahib had deep bayonet wounds and a massive sword cut across his face.

Savages! Lalbahadur muttered, the incident still vivid memory. He would never give in to these barbarians, and would see that none of his men did so either. Not that he expected them to, and in this he was right.

He opened his eyes at the sound of a voice. Watanabe's servant was standing in front of the subedar with a dish of rice and curry. Lalbahadur could smell the delicious aroma. 'The Nippon Captain says you are a brave man, and in honour he sends you this meal.'

Lalbahadur looked at the dish before him, then across to the bungalow where Watanabe was standing on the verandah. And he noticed that there seemed to be more Japanese guards around doing nothing. He knew at once that the meal would not be as appetising as it promised. But to refuse it would probably have worse repercussions than accepting.

He moulded some rice and curry into a ball with his fingers and managed to flick it into his aching mouth with the thumb. The curry must have contained at least a handful of the little, red-hot chillies because the heat in his mouth was like a jungle fire. Great beads of sweat broke out on his forehead and his eyes watered. With a great effort he swallowed and felt the meal going down like lava from a volcano.

The captain had come forward to the verandah steps, the guards were beginning to grin, but Lalbahadur rolled another ball of rice and curry and popped it into his mouth. He needed all his reserves of courage to finish the meal. His tongue was tender and aflame, his eyes red and his head ached. But the expression on the faces of the guards was a sign of his triumph – an even greater one when Watanabe returned angrily inside his bungalow. Lalbahadur tensed in anticipation of an army of guards descending on him to administer another beating, but no one came near him.

Jemadar Deobahadur, watching from the doorway of his hut, said desperately, 'He cannot stay there any longer. He needs attention. He must come back to the hut.'

'It will bring trouble to us all if we move him,' Jemadar Hariprasad said.

'What talk is this?' Deobahadur snapped. 'Are we all cowards?'

Hariprasad drew back as though struck a blow. He it was who had single-handed destroyed a Jap tank with a Molotov Cocktail north of Kuala Lumpur, blocking the narrow loop road, and giving the battalion vital time to move back to a stronger position. 'Do you accuse me of cowardice?' he asked.

'I? No, of course not, not personally. I was referring to all of us if we do not do something for the Subedar Sahib.'

'And what do you suggest?'

'Either we bring him back in here now and give him water, or we must ask the Nippon captain to allow us to do so.'

'And either way is like tackling a wounded tiger.'

Lalbahadur still sat in the sun, his mouth felt a bit better, as though the jungle fire was beginning to come under control. But not as bad, he consoled himself, as that time in 1915 when he had been wounded at Vital Point in Mesopotamia, when General Townshend Sahib had been in command, he who later surrendered at Kut. There followed that terrible ride in the springless cart, every bump raking his wound, shivering in the drastic drop of temperature at night, but his mouth afire with thirst like so many of his wounded companions who cried out for water but there was not enough to go round. Had he cried that night? A mere boy at the time, and maybe he

110

had.

He certainly felt like crying now. But this time it was different; he had a responsibility to bear, and a dangerous game to play with Watanabe, one side carrying all the heavy weapons, the other just the honour that must not be tarnished.

'Sahib. Sahib!' Deobahadur cried suddenly close to him. 'We are taking you back to the hut.'

Lalbahadur allowed himself to be lifted to his feet before he said anxiously: 'Wait! Have you permission?'

'Yes, Subedar Sahib,' Hariprasad calmed him.

They helped him into the hut and stretched him out on the matting which served as a bed. He was given water which he sipped slowly; not hosing his mouth like a fireman to put out the fire but slowly, each drop to be savoured.

'I still do not know how you persuaded Watanabe,' he said when he felt better.

'We bowed and grovelled,' Hariprasad looked sorely ashamed. 'And he said that he would only let you go if we agreed to join the INA.'

Lalbahadur sat up abruptly, wincing with pain. 'No!'

'Steady, Sahib. Do you think that of us?'

'Well?'

'We explained why we could not do that because of our most solemn oath of loyalty to the British King. For a moment I thought he would have us executed on the spot. Instead he said, "You Gurkhas are very brave – but stupid. Take your Subedar Sahib." '

'And you were not beaten?'

'No violence at all,' Hariprasad confirmed.

'I do not like it.' Lalbahadur was puzzled. 'He must be planning something, some terrible torture, to try and break us.'

'We will not break,' Deobahadur said stoutly.

By nightfall no more had been seen of Captain Watanabe. The others felt relieved, but Lalbahadur could not sleep. He was not worried for himself, but the thought of Deobahadur and Hariprasad and the rest being subjected to brutal treatment disturbed him greatly.

He had fallen asleep eventually, but was aroused with a start as Japanese soldiers stormed the hut, butts clubbing, kicking, forcing the Gurkhas outside. Daylight was just brightening the sky as the Gurkha officers were bundled into the back of closed trucks which then drove out of the camp at speed. About half an hour later the trucks halted at the barbed-wire garlanded gates of a large building. The gates were opened and the trucks driven through into the compound where the tailboards were let down with a crash. A gang of Jap bully boys turned the prisoners out, helped with blows from bamboo canes. 'Out! Out! Out! Double! Double! Double!' They were forced to run about a mile to shabby huts. And there they were left in Jap fashion to wait unheeded for several hours.

Lalbahadur realized that a far higher command than Watanabe was responsible for the instruction to beat the Gurkhas into submission. In the hut he met several Gurkha officers from the 1st, 2nd and 9th Gurkha Rifles. All had already been beaten for refusing to join the INA, and as old hands suspected that what had happened so far was nothing to the monster of brutality obviously lying in wait.

If the Gurkhas, long revered as Britain's most loyal comrades in arms, were to renege on their oath and join the INA it would be a considerable Japanese victory. Lalbahadur was sure that the Japs would try every foul trick and tough persuasion to achieve this end. He was still confident that his riflemen would resist; his anxiety was that they might suffer as a consequence, especially without the presence of their own officers. But he comforted himself by deciding that the Japs would first concentrate on the Gurkha officers.

After a long wait, the Jap bully boys reappeared to force march them to the large building where they were segregated in pairs, each to a cell. Lalbahadur found himself with young Deobahadur. They waited again for what seemed hours, the older man trying his best to keep the younger one calm. Then the door was opened and an armed guard escorted them to a large room where a Jap officer stood menacingly in the middle, booted legs apart, one hand on hip, the other on the hilt of his sword.

He remained in this position as another Jap addressed the pair. There was the usual rhetoric about Imperial pigs, desertion by the British officers, how India would soon be free, and as members of the INA they would be heroes and have important positions in the new Indian National Army which would be raised.

Lalbahadur wanted to laugh at the crass ignorance shown of the Gurkhas' background. Their reputation as fighting men was well known, but it was amazing how ignorant the Japanese seemed to be about Nepal's political and geographical relationship with India. The Japanese were even using a language foreign to both, instead of finding a Gurkhali speaker.

At last came the moment Lalbahadur was dreading, as once again he had to explain that the Gurkhas were not indigenous to India. They came from Nepal, an Independent Kingdom in the Himalayas. They were in a sense mercenaries, but different in that they had sworn allegiance to the British Sovereign, and the Gurkhas always kept a solemn promise. He did not say it to the Jap – although he thought it wryly for a moment – but the Gurkhas did not receive the largess mercenaries usually enjoyed.

The Japanese officer, on being told what Lalbahadur had replied, moved his hand from his hip and clicked his fingers. At once three burly Japs descended on Deobahadur, beating him with bamboo canes, then hitting him with their fists until he was on his knees and finally collapsed into unconsciousness. One of the Japs gave him the customary kick in the ribs as he lay there.

The translator said to Lalbahadur, 'If you want him spared any further punishment, and your men likewise, you must agree to join the INA.'

'He would not want me to dishonour his name. And I would not wish to bring disgrace to any of my men. We are POWs and should be treated as such.'

'Japanese Army does not recognize prisoners. Japanese soldiers would rather die than be taken prisoners. You are nothing.'

'Then why do you want us for the INA?'

The next moment he was being brutally beaten and as he slipped into unconsciousness he thought that he was passing over into death.

When he recovered consciousness a few minutes later, it was only to be beaten senseless again, as was Deobahadur. This happened a third time, before they were dragged back to the cell, and thrown in, and the door locked. Lalbahadur and young Deobahadur had never known such pain, but a short time later the door opened and a British POW doctor came in to give them what treatment he could, which was limited. To the best of his belief there were no broken bones. 'They bring an art to it,' he said. 'Maximum pain, but no physical damage at this stage. The swine. Although God alone knows what you will suffer later.'

Their ordeal was not yet over; there was another session of beatings before, a few days later, the Gurkha officers were suddenly loaded up into the trucks and driven back to their POW camps. All bore witness to the severe beatings they had suffered. Some had been unfortunate and had broken limbs, some internal injuries, but not one had yielded.

The Japanese realizing that they were not going to break the GOs, turned their attention to the NCOs. It was again an anxious time for the Gurkha officers, but their NCOs, although suffering torture, also remained loyal to their salt. By then the Japs knew that they would never persuade the Gurkhas to join the INA, so they split them up as much as possible, all over South-East Asia, where, without any GOs to help them, many suffered dreadfully at the hands of brutal Jap guards.

For those who remained in the main camp it was a hard time, as it was for all POWs, although they were not engaged on the Death Railway – a degradation reserved for Europeans and Australians.

As the months passed, life in the prison camp settled into a routine of back-breaking coolie labour, and a constant worry about food and medicine. The Gurkhas learned the tricks to deceive the Jap guards, to obtain extras from the Chinese outside the prison fence. Lalbahadur also found that he could win more for his men now that Watanabe no longer had to attempt to force them to join the INA, and even showed signs of respect at the courage displayed by the Gurkhas. But it was a knife-edged relationship which Lalbahadur had to learn to walk without falling down a precipice of beatings or executions.

One day the British officers managed to make contact. It was a momentous occasion. Major Hutton of the 2/15th smuggled himself into a fatigue party of British other ranks working near the Gurkha camp, and was able to speak to

Lalbahadur through the fence. It almost broke the middle-aged subedar's heart to see the normally dapper major sahib, who had so prided himself on his immaculate appearance, wearing a pair of khaki shorts which were only just decent, and a vest which must have belonged to a saint.

Hutton on his part was deeply distressed by the terrible marks left on the subedar's face as evidence of the severe beatings and torture he had suffered, and by the limp which would be permanent. And God knows whether he had sustained any internal injuries which had yet to make themselves manifest. At the same time, Hutton was proud of the subedar's turn out – well-worn clothes, maybe, but clean and still bearing the semblance of a uniform.

'You must tell me the name of your tailor, Subedar Sahib.'

Lalbahadur wanted to smile. The major sahib was always one for a joke, but he felt tears in his eyes instead. How easy it had become to weep at the least excuse.

'How are the men?'

'No need for the Major Sahib to worry. We will survive.'

'Have you enough money? No, do not answer that because I know you of old, Lalbahadur. I will see if I can get some Straits dollars to you, but not much or the Japs might get suspicious.'

He looked round sharply. 'I must go.' And left at once to rejoin the fatigue party.

Lalbahadur stared at the empty space on the other side of the fence for quite a while, thinking of the past, wondering of the future.

The months went by, each one increasing the hardships as food became scarce and medicinal supplies like gold dust. Lalbahadur watched over his men, using all his cunning to prevent them becoming listless or depressed, to finding ways of improving the food supply which was not easy. The GOs were given a meagre pay of thirty Straits dollars a month, while the other ranks received money only for actual work done, and then seldom as much as half a dollar a day. Thankfully the savage beatings had stopped, although Lalbahadur always had to watch out for the Jap bully boys who were ever on the look out for ways of satisfying their sadistic bents.

Many of the British officers, he knew, had been sent to the atrocious Death Railway. And when he heard in December 1943 that survivors from the Gurkha Brigade officers had returned, he was anxious to know how many of his battalion's officers were among them. So he went out with a fatigue party collecting building material. A group from the British camp was working nearby. Lalbahadur indicated to a bored guard that he was going to relieve himself. He stepped behind the ruins of what had been quite a good hotel, and a moment later Major Hutton joined him. The subedar was shaken at the major's appearance, even more so than the time he had spoken to him at the camp. Hutton had become pitifully thin, eyes embedded, clothes reduced to a loincloth.

'I am glad to see you back, Major Sahib,' the subedar managed to say, choking back his emotions.

'What there is of me,' Hutton replied, trying to smile.

'We must not be too long,' Lalbahadur warned, both knew they could be executed if discovered. 'But tell me of the other Sahibs.'

'I am afraid we lost Lieutenant Thompson and Captain Grant. You have no idea of the conditions we worked in. I think Thompson Sahib just gave up and died. Grant Sahib had malaria and dysentery. Poor man, he suffered terribly before he died – there was not enough medicine available. But the rest of us managed to get back.'

Hutton spared Lalbahadur the full gruesome details of those nightmare months on the Death Railway. It would not do the subedar's morale any good, and he had enough to worry about already.

One of Lalbahadur's greatest anxieties concerned Jemadar Deobahadur, the young Gurkha officer who had suffered those terrible beatings alongside him. Deobahadur must have received some serious internal injury which had taken a little while to reveal itself, but there was nothing the POW doctor could do, either to make an accurate diagnosis or to effect a cure.

Deobahadur had been so fit and strong that he took a long time dying. As the months went past he grew thinner, his face yellow and pinched. Suddenly he looked an old man, all the proud muscles wasted away. Even the Japs realized that they could not get any more work out of him, and he spent his days lying on a mat in the hut. Lalbahadur tried to keep his spirits up, talking of the future, of how the war would have to end soon, that Britain and America would destroy the Japs before long. But even D-Day in Europe, which sent a thrill of excitement down the spine of nearly every POW when the news flashed around the camp, brought only a flicker of Deobahadur's eyelids.

As the pain grew worse, it grieved Lalbahadur to see the thin, wasted body racked in agony, and the end, when it came, did so quite suddenly. He was holding the young Gurkha's hand, like father and son, indeed he had begun to look upon Deobahadur as his own son for he himself had only sired daughters. He was telling Deobahadur about the old days in the regiment when he felt the young man's life slip away out of his hands. He released the lifeless hand and closed the half staring eyes. Then he wept.

But it was the last time that he did so, even when other Gurkhas died in the final year of captivity, mainly through lack of proper medical treatment and food. By that time he considered all of them as sons to be cared for in every way, but there was no sorrow left in him, only a cold anger and the hope that somehow Captain Watanabe and his kind, many of them a great deal more brutal and sadistic, would be meted out just punishment. He knew that conventions would forbid the Japs from getting a taste of their own medicine, but hang they would.

He could sense a change in the Jap guards who were beginning to realize that all was not going so well for the Japanese Empire. And on Guy Fawkes Day 1944, the Allies staged their own fireworks display by bombing Singapore Naval Base with fifty bombers, definite proof that the fight back had begun. But great care had still to be taken. Lalbahadur knew he must be wary, the Japs were quite capable of exterminating witnesses, even to the extent of a blood-bath, as indeed happened to many Gurkhas in Java.

Secret wireless sets told of the recapture of Burma, and the days waiting for the British to land in Malaya seemed longer and more drawn out than the three years that had passed.

'If only they would parachute arms for us,' Jemadar Hariprasad said. 'We could slaughter the bastards now.'

'You had your moment of glory with that tank,' Lalbahadur

117

said. 'And since then, you have shown courage and tact in captivity, a great help to me in my task. Do not waste it all at the last minute, do not reveal your feelings by even the slightest lapse to the Jap guards. They have itchy trigger fingers now. We have only to hold out a bit longer.'

'I am sorry, Subedar Sahib, but my loathing for them is so great.'

Lalbahadur touched his arm. 'I understand. But it will be worth the wait. And you will be a much better officer for the experience gained.'

News came through that Japan had capitulated on 14 August 1945, but there was still a frustrating wait in a vacuum of anxiety until early in September when the gates were opened and the British officers entered the camp to greet their men in complete freedom. And the men responded in typical Gurkha fashion – drawn up on parade in a hotchpotch of clothes which were still as smart as any uniform. It brought a lump to Major Hutton's throat, more than any other form of welcome could have done, to see the men on parade, and Subedar Lalbahadur Gurung marching up to salute and report that the 2nd Battalion of the 15th Gurkha Rifles was ready for inspection.

There was a mist before Hutton's eyes. 'I think, Subedar Sahib, before you unman us completely, that you had better dismiss the parade, and let us then all join together as old friends.'

If Captain Watanabe could have heard this conversation, and seen the men on parade, he might at last have realized why it was that the Gurkhas had withstood the savage beatings and tortures rather than break their solemn oaths, and why they had remained loyal to their British officers and the British Crown.

But Captain Watanabe and his men were already having their own taste of prison camp, and the shadow of the hangman's noose was over many of them.

The Scorpion Trap

The sapper company had worked all through the hot, Burmese day preparing the three centre spans of the Sittang Bridge for demolition. But more than 3,000 British, Indian, Gurkha and Burmese troops of the 17th Indian Division were still trapped on the far side of the mile wide river, caught in a running battle with the Japanese.

Nothing seemed to be going right for Major-General Jackie Smyth VC. Each crack of a rifle, each staccato burst from a machine-gun was like a rivet being driven into his body. Yet it could have been so different. He had said so to himself enough times in the past weeks, like a gramophone needle stuck in a groove that went on and on. But when at last the soundbox was given a nudge out of the groove it was too late, and now he knew with absolute finality that there was nothing more he could do except sit it out.

As darkness fell on 22 February 1942, the general, faint from lack of food, weary in mind and body – a body which he had kept so fit throughout his career and now threatened to let him down at this most vital moment of his life – at last drove back to his Operations HQ some seven miles west of the bridge. A bite to eat and a few hours sleep were needed to revitalize him, to help him fight the pain.

But it seemed as though he had hardly closed his eyes when he was awakened to take an urgent telephone call from Brigadier Hugh-Jones, the bridgehead commander. As the general was handed the receiver he sensed that his worst fear was about to be realized. He had, after all, stressed to Hugh-Jones that on no account must the enemy seize the bridge intact.

Hugh-Jones reported, 'I have had a word with Captain Orgill of the Malerkotla Field Company, and if the bridge is not blown now he cannot guarantee to do so in the morning.'

'Why is that?' Smyth asked.

'There's not enough fuse and electric cable. He's had to locate the firing point on the bridge itself, some distance from the west bank. And now the Japs have established a machine-gun post on the railway cutting. We've tried to dislodge it. We made determined and costly attempts but we failed.' He added that probing bursts were ricocheting off the girders, so in daylight the sappers would be dangerously exposed when they touched off the fuses.

Smyth wondered if Hugh-Jones had spoken to the commanders of the bridgehead troops, and the brigadier confirmed that he had. 'Both are of the same mind, sir. Our bridgehead is holding off the enemy at the moment, but a more concentrated attack in the morning is inevitable, and if the bridge is to be destroyed successfully it must be under cover of darkness.'

Smyth lowered the receiver, holding it against his chest. The enemy could have bombed the bridge at any time, but it was much more important to them intact as the shortest route to Rangoon. If the bridge was not destroyed, two Japanese divisions would march straight into Rangoon virtually unopposed, precipitating the fall of Burma and placing India in a grave position.

On the other hand, some two thirds of his division were still on the wrong side of the river. Wireless communications had broken down, but obviously his men were fighting desperately to breach the block the enemy had established between them and the Sittang Railway Bridge, which was the only way across the Sittang for miles.

The iron bridge was 500 yards long, of eleven spans, each 150 feet, and recently decked over to take road traffic and marching troops. The river widened below the bridge to 1,000 yards, a formidable obstacle even to strong swimmers because of the treacherous current and the forty foot rise and fall of the tide. So many of his troops were non-swimmers, or hardly proficient to make the crossing. And there were no boats, certainly not since the previous day when some 300 sampans had been bought by the Royal Engineers from Burmese villagers on both side of the river, and destroyed to deny their use by the enemy.

What a hopeless situation. He was caught with his division split, the enemy attacking fiercely, and the bridge still intact. And what a horrible decision to make, Smyth thought. He had gone over the pros and cons many times and knew that there was really only one conclusion to reach. But he hesitated, allowing himself another five minutes of deliberation, seeking despairingly for an alternative solution.

☆   ☆   ☆

Across the river, on the east bank, Brigadier Jones of 16th Brigade had, the previous evening, set up a defence position around Mokpalin village, about a mile south of the bridge. The perimeter was manned by a mixed bag of units from the division's three brigades which had dispersed in the confusion caused by the surprise Jap attacks that morning.

One of the units was C Company of the 1/15th Gurkha Rifles, commanded by Second-Lieutenant Bruce Stevens. Separated from his battalion when it was ambushed, he had led his men to Mokpalin where Brigadier Jones had allotted a position for his company on the perimeter, linking up with the other units, most of them under strength, some down to a company – The Duke's, KOYLI, three Gurkha battalions, one of Jats, two from the Burma Rifles, and the remnants of a Dogra battalion. There were also three Indian Mountain Artillery Batteries, and 5 Field Battery RA.

On reaching his allotted area, Bruce quickly set the men to work. Two platoons defending the front line dug in amongst a line of bushes and broken bamboo fences. He placed his HQ a short distance inside the perimeter, beyond a narrow, village track and near a small, wooden house, together with his third platoon held in reserve.

By nightfall the Gurkhas were well dug in, relieved to be part of an organised defence and to be making a stand, and very alert, knowing how swiftly the Japs could launch their attacks.

Bruce waited at his HQ, nerves tingling in anticipation of what the night might bring, how many more men he would lose. A month ago he had eighty, now he had fewer than fifty. He was only nineteen years old, an Emergency Commission

Officer short on military experience, but propelled into command when his company commander was killed by the first shots he had heard fired in anger. That had been one month and some 300 miles ago at Kawkareik when the Japs invaded Burma across the Thai border. Since then, 17th Division had withdrawn steadily towards Rangoon, through Kawkareik, Moulmein, the Salween, Martaban, up the Lower Burma coastline to Bilin River where Smyth had to make a three day stand before receiving permission to break contact and race for the Sittang Bridge.

But unknown to Smyth, when withdrawing from Bilin, one of his units gave out its orders in clear and the message was picked up by the enemy. For Lieutenant-General Sakurai, commanding the élite Japanese 33rd Division, it was a marvellous opportunity to cut off the British from the Sittang Bridge. Knowing Smyth's line of withdrawal, the Japanese general was able to set a scorpion trap – the old favourite Japanese manoeuvre established in ancient times. The Japanese infantry was like a scorpion with claws outstretched, reaching to seize its prey from behind so that it could be held and stung to death.

Acting on Sakurai's immediate orders, 215th Regiment moved out into the night of 19 February; around 5,000 ruthless and experienced soldiers advancing at top speed along cross-country tracks, through the dense Burmese jungle, hungry for more action and victory. Once 17th Division was held in their grasp like some fragile grasshopper, the rest of the Japanese 33rd Division, together with the 55th, would be ready to give the death sting.

The 17th Indian Division was in the process of crossing the river on the morning of 22 February, vehicles and men spread over fifteen miles from the bridgehead back along the dusty track that passed as a road, when the Japanese 215th Regiment arrived. The bridgehead stood firm throughout the long, hot day. Further back, 48th, 16th and 46th Brigades had been thrown into confusion by the lack of contact with Division HQ. The 48th Brigade made an attempt to break out through the Jap infiltrators and reach the bridgehead. As more enemy soldiers arrived, the 46th Brigade was ambushed and split into small units. So it was that by nightfall of 22 February, about a third of the division was across the river, and manning the bridgehead, others were lost in the jungle, and the largest group was prepared to defend itself in the village of Mokpalin.

Bruce wondered how many Japs were out there beyond the perimeter, forming up in the jungle, on the scrub slopes, in the *chaungs*, hidden in folds in the ground, no doubt amply equipped with artillery and mortars. He had no information on the enemy's actual strength, but he guessed that at least two divisions were closing in for the kill.

'Let us take a last look around the position,' he said to Subedar Tilbir Rana, his second-in-command, on whose experience and sound advice he relied. The subedar was a quietly spoken man in his late thirties, giving an impression of softness. But his soft, brown eyes could change in an instant to the paralysing glitter of a snake's eyes, making tough Gurkha NCOs wish the ground would open to devour them, and young riflemen wish they were back in their snowy mountains of Nepal if they had made some foolish error.

Bruce and Tilbir walked forward the short distance from HQ to where 13 and 15 Platoons waited. Just thirty-two men in all, but alert, anxious for the action to start, and by now well experienced and confident in their ability to match the Japs in straight contest. Bruce encouraged the men, and made sure that they would not fire on automatic unless absolutely necessary. Hand-grenades and cold steel would be the order of the night. The Gurkhas were excited, and their morale was high in spite of all they had been through, and what was to come.

He returned with Tilbir to his HQ, and at once sensed that something was about to break, a feeling like being locked in a cupboard with no air, suffocating in the great hate that surrounded him. Then the dark night was rent apart by artillery flashes. Exploding shells reverberated around the perimeter, mortar bombs dropping in from their high trajectory found victims about a hundred yards away in another unit – Bruce could hear their screams and shouts. Fierce machine-gun fire opened up from the north, east and south, the tracer threading the darkness with stitches of red, green and white to indicate the various Japanese unit formations. There was also the usual rattle of cracker guns to try and locate the defenders' machine-gun positions.

Then the first line of infantry hit the perimeter in groups of fifteen, armed with bayonets, swords, grenades and supported by LMGs, rising like apparitions out of the ground a short distance in front of Bruce's forward platoons, having crawled forward under cover of the artillery barrage. The Gurkhas remained calm, meeting the enemy with steady fire and a flurry of hand-grenades. The air seemed filled with the grenades of both sides, thrown or propelled by discharger cups, breaking up, segments flying in all directions. All around the village the noise reached a crescendo as every soldier fought stubbornly to hold back the enemy.

Bruce wanted to rush forward to help his platoons, but knew he must stay firm. They could be relied upon, they knew what they were doing. Then a mortar bomb exploded quite close, followed quickly by another and still another, the shrapnel rattling among the trees like children running sticks along railings. Behind him there was a brighter flare of light as a bomb exploded among his reserve platoon. There were cries of pain, but he had to wait, he couldn't investigate at once.

And then, almost as suddenly as they had attacked, the Japs withdrew, obviously to reform, badly mauled in their first attempt to take Mokpalin. Now Bruce was able to rush over to his reserve platoon where he found three dead, one seriously wounded and the rest shaken. Bruce said to Havildar Bharti Gurung, 14 Platoon Commander: 'Take the wounded man to the aid post. You know where it is?'

'Huzoor.'

When Bharti and a stretcher party had gone, Bruce had the three dead men carried behind some bushes, out of sight for the moment, and laid out properly. Then he went forward to find out how his other platoons had fared. Amazingly there were no casualties, and every man remained at a high pitch of excitement, but Jemadar Thandraj Gurung of 13 Platoon whispered, 'Be careful, Sahib, they are still out there, waiting for the next attack. A bigger one this time, I think.'

And he was right. It was around 22.00 hours, starting with the same build up of artillery and mortars. In the distance, where the road wound its way back towards the Mokpalin Quarries, there was a line of flame as many of the division's abandoned lorries were set alight. An ammunition truck blew up in a billowing balloon of flame that scorched the night air, and made the ground tremble.

Towards C Company's front the Japs came in again, chattering to each other, and were soon locked in hand-to-hand combat with the Gurkhas. Screams punctuated the night, shouts of rage, cries of terror. Through the struggling figures came more helmeted troops, breaking through into Company Headquarters.

Bruce had his rifle and bayonet to hand. His orderly, Gopiram, was by his side and ready to guard his sahib to the death. Bruce leapt out of his weapon pit, rifle at the port, then down, straight and firm. The approaching Jap bared his teeth as he plunged forward; Bruce met him, bayonet to bayonet, held him back, forced through his enemy's guard. He withdrew the blade cleanly, the dead man falling away to his left, mouth open for a scream that was never made. Now Bruce swung the rifle round to bring up the butt with savage ferocity into the yelling face of a second Jap, felling him to the ground in a lifeless heap. Out of the corner of his eye he glimpsed yet another enemy soldier bearing down on him, bayonet an arm's length away. Then Gopiram was there, his kukri slashing the man into oblivion.

The rest of the headquarters men were also fighting for their lives. A Gurkha went down, his head cut open by a swinging sword. Then Subedar Tilbir was into the Japs, the kukri was in the hand of a master as he brought it into deadly effect like a whirling whip of steel that was soon red with blood.

The Japs gave way all along the perimeter, the survivors retreating, followed by a bombardment from 5 Field Battery RA, and the 3.7 inch howitzers of the 28th Indian Mountain Regiment who, earlier, had been firing over open sights, cutting a wide swathe in the enemy's ranks.

And so the night passed. No long moments for a man really to recover his breath; and all through the night, further back, the British and Indian doctors were working by flashlight as the wounded mounted in numbers, doing what they could, realizing surely the futility of it all.

Bruce's mouth was dry, his eyes burned, his uniform stuck to his body with sweat and grime. It was about 5.30, soon be dawn, but would daylight bring only more attacks, and how much longer could they hold out?

He was mulling this over in his mind when a blinding flash of light and a blast of red-hot air caught the village in a grip, and behind it came the roar of the explosion, and he knew that the Sittang Bridge had been blown.

And as the bridge sagged drunkenly into the river there was a strange, brief hush. A moment of silence, like an armistice for the dead.

☆　☆　☆

A heavyweight boxer could not have delivered a harder, more energy sapping punch, Bruce thought. The aftermath of the explosion had left him dazed and sick in the stomach. The trap was closed; now the Japs had them in the grip of the scorpion's claws and were ready to apply the killing sting.

Around him, Bruce sensed that all his men were stunned; and probably everyone on the east side of the river must have felt the same terror, anger, bewilderment. For the strong swimmers like himself the obstacle was not insurmountable, but for the Gurkhas the blowing up of the bridge had clearly sentenced them to death or capture.

Not one of them could swim. And this applied to all the Gurkha regiments, apart from a few men here and there.

Bruce shouted, 'Do not worry. I will get you all across the river. Somehow I will, I promise you.'

How did his men take it? Did they believe him? There was no time to find out because the silence was broken by Japanese cries of rage, echoing across the hills and the river, and the crash of their artillery signalled a fresh onslaught, a determination to tear the British defences apart. This was the time for frightened men to break, to panic, but his Gurkhas held firm, as all around the perimeter the other Gurkhas, Jats, Dogras, the ravaged ranks of the Duke of Wellington's, and the sturdy Yorkshiremen from the King's Own Yorkshire Light Infantry, held firm.

As daylight finally pushed aside the night which seemed never-ending, the stark evidence of the battle lay revealed. The Japs had fought frantically, leaving many of their bodies in front of the perimeter. Within Bruce's own section the bodies of those Japs who had managed to infiltrate

126

still lay in the dust. Near them were his own dead. The cheerful, portly, quartermaster-havildar looked reprovingly out of sightless eyes, a signaller had been cut from head to groin, and the company havildar-major who had made the enemy pay dearly for his life. In 13 and 15 Platoons holding the perimeter, five had been killed and three badly wounded. Adding the casualties already suffered by 14 Platoon, the total was eleven killed and four wounded.

By now the Japs had pulled back after their last attack. Whether they would come again, Bruce was not certain. Now that the bridge was destroyed there was little point in continuing the onslaught on Mokpalin, especially as they had themselves suffered heavy casualties. The enemy's most important task, surely, he thought, was to find an alternative crossing point further north to continue their advance on Rangoon.

In the lull, the wounded were taken back to the casualty aid post. There was time to bury the Gurkha dead, and to tidy up the Jap corpses. And the word came that Brigadier Jones intended to disperse the force at 20.30 hours and attempt to get as many men as possible across the river.

The silence continued for several hours until shortly before midday there was the drone of approaching aircraft, coming into sight like small blodges, expanding rapidly into more than a score of Jap bombers, their bombs setting several houses alight, and finding targets among the abandoned vehicles. A gun ammunition truck exploded, discharging black smoke streaked with red flashes into the sky, and hurling shrapnel in all directions. The bombers moved away, slowly becoming smaller and smaller before disappearing from view, leaving behind many casualties, but Bruce's company had escaped any hits.

Bruce visited his men in their positions. He wondered if their mouths were as dry as his, if their eyes were as weary as his, if they were afraid of the immediate future as he was. He felt really exhausted, but tried not to show it, which took a great effort and probably was not worth it because the Gurkhas must damn well know how he felt.

'What is the water situation?' he asked Thandraj of 13 Platoon.

'Not too good, Sahib.' The jemadar took off his Gurkha hat

and ran a hand over his shaven head which was wet with sweat. 'I have tried to impress on them the importance of drinking sparingly. Maybe each man has about a quarter of a bottle left, some less, some maybe more. The *chagals* we still have (he was referring to the canvas water carriers) and I keep those near me.'

The other platoon was in a similar situation. 'I know we have no food left,' Bruce said. 'But do you think some hot tea would help? Using some of that water reserve.'

'We will make tea, Sahib,' Thandraj said.

'I should do it now before the Japs decide to pay us another visit.'

'They will not be invited to our tea party, Sahib,' Thandraj said with a broad grin, which in itself was a morale booster for Bruce.

He returned to his HQ and made the same suggestion to Subedar Tilbir. And when he took a sip from the mug of hot sweet tea Gopiram brought him, he felt better. But the nightmare of what was to come stayed with him.

The day passed slowly, the sun swung across the bowl of the sky, building up the heat. Then in the early afternoon came word that the brigadier had decided to bring forward the withdrawal immediately, units to make their way independently to the river.

Bruce called his platoon commanders together. 'Can anyone swim?' he asked optimistically. They shook their heads. 'Then I suppose we will have to make some rafts. There is quite a lot of wood in that house behind us. We will carry as much as possible down to the river. And any bamboo we can find. And while that is being done I want to check up on our wounded. We have four of our men at the aid post.'

'Will we take them with us?' Tilbir asked.

'I should like to try. What do you think?'

'Yes. We must try. There will be little hope for them after we have gone and the Japs find them.'

'All right. Bharti, I shall take your platoon. Meanwhile, Subedar Sahib, will you carry on here, gather the wood, get the men ready to move down to the river when I return.'

As he led Bharti's platoon towards the aid post, there was gunfire in the distance. Some of the houses and the transport packed inside the village were still burning. Black, smelly smoke, and burning bamboo exploding like rifle fire.

The fumes made him cough as he scrambled through the wreckage, past several bodies, the weapons of the dead and wounded lying all over the place, until he found Captain Green – who was always called Doc – a tall, thin man with large, boney hands which somehow were able to bring comfort by their touch. He was the 1/15th's MO, but had joined up with other regimental doctors to form an emergency aid post in the village because the Advance Dressing Station of 39 Field Ambulance, and the Assistant and Deputy Directors of Medical Services, had been captured the previous day.

'Glad to see you still in one piece,' Doc said.

'Thanks, Doc. We're moving out now.'

'Best of luck, Bruce.' He looked vague, worn down by fatigue, he must have been operating all night, doing what he could for the wounded.

'Aren't you coming with us?' Bruce asked.

'With you?' Doc looked puzzled.

'The Japs will be here soon.'

'Thanks for the thought, Bruce, but I've got to stay with the wounded. There's still so much to be done.'

Bruce realized that Doc had made up his mind. 'OK Doc, you must do what you think best. But I would like to take my four wounded men with me if you are agreeable.'

'They are here, Sahib,' Bharti called out.

'Let's have a look,' Doc said, 'I don't suppose any of them should be moved, but I guess they'd have just as much chance with you.'

Bharti's men quickly lifted the wounded Gurkhas on their stretchers. One of the men cried out in pain. Bharti spoke softly to him. The youngest Gurkha in the company opened his eyes. 'I could not help myself, Havildar Sahib. I will try not to cry out again.' He closed his eyes.

'Goodbye, Doc,' Bruce called out, but the doctor was already deep in the examination of yet another wounded man.

It was with real sadness that Bruce turned away, knowing that the chances of his meeting the Doc again were very slim. As they began to leave the aid post, Bruce felt like someone who had gone into the Battersea Dogs' Home and come out with one dog, and could feel all the other eyes looking at him appealingly, crying out to be taken as well. The other wounded were not crying out, but Bruce could feel their eyes on him, and the very silence of their appeal seemed to be the loudest sound he had ever heard.

Shit! How could he take them all? He wasn't sure how he was going to get his company across, much less the wounded. But he knew he had to try. He turned back to Doc, and managed to attract his attention. 'Are there any others who may have a chance?'

Doc looked at him for a moment, and Bruce thought he was going to refuse out of hand. But the Doc moved quickly among the wounded and pointed out four more. 'That's the lot. They may live if you can cross the river on wings.'

'Water-wings, Doc,' Bruce said.

'What! Go on, clear off.' But he added softly, 'When the war is over remind me to buy you a drink.'

Bruce had sent Gopiram to collect more men and now there were enough to carry the eight wounded, including two from the KOYLI and two from the Duke's, back to the company's position. There Bruce found that a great deal of the house had been dismantled and the men were ready to move. He led the way out of the village with a section from Thandraj's platoon. The timber and pieces of bamboo were spread out as loads among the men as it had been decided to wait till they reached the river before attempting to make rafts.

The smoke was quite thick now, forming an excellent screen, enabling them to make their way unobserved, while exploding ammunition was loud and fearsome enough to form a rampart which the enemy hesitated to approach too close. Bruce did not know at the time that this was due to some splendid and unselfish work by men from the 2/5th Royal Gurkha Rifles and the 1/9th Royal Jat Regiment.

There were shouts coming from all around, disembodied voices in the smoke and jungle, and firing had renewed on the far perimeter. The Indian Mountain Batteries were also fighting fiercely with shrapnel, fuse O, having a devastating effect at short range.

The Gurkha company crossed the railway line, climbed beyond it past huts and trees for about a quarter of a mile. There was a lot of noise ahead, and Bruce halted the column.

I am going to patrol forward to the cliff's edge,' he told Tilbir.

'I think I must come with you, Sahib.'

So Bruce, Tilbir, Gopiram and a couple of riflemen from the leading section, moved carefully to the edge of the cliff, and from the cover of some thick shrubs looked down onto the river.

The sight which met his eyes would be with Bruce forever. Hundreds of British, Gurkha, Indian and Burmese troops were packed tight along the beach like Brighton on a Bank Holiday. Only there was no happy laughter, no frolicking in the water. Out on that beach were many dangerous men because they were leaderless, hungry, exhausted, wounded, very frightened. But there were others who showed courage and leadership, organising groups to cross the river in or on just about everything that could float: planks, logs, water-bottles, petrol tins, bamboo, *chagals* blown up like Mae Wests, all made into some sort of raft or lifebelt. Most of the soldiers had abandoned their weapons. Like litter after a football match, rifles, tommy-guns, Brens, mortars, revolvers, hand-grenades were strewn along the river's edge. Many of the men had discarded most of their clothes, and quite a few were naked to improve their chances when attempting to swim the treacherous river which now, at full tide, stretched a muddy green colour for one and a half miles to the distant bank.

The river was already full of bobbing heads. In some units officers were maintaining good discipline, keeping their men close together, taking as many weapons as possible on improvised rafts, the swimmers helping the non-swimmers. Many who could swim a few lengths of a swimming pool found the width of the river too much for their strength and were swept away by the current or just vanished beneath the water. In a few miraculous cases, men carried out to sea by the current floated back with the tide. It was also a time for many heroes, supporting friends who could not swim; the strong swimmers crossing the river two or three times to take the wounded over on makeshift rafts; men giving up their places on rafts for wounded comrades.

The cliff afforded some protection, but now and then a Jap sniper found a target, a bobbing head disappearing in a froth of blood. Pockets of 17th Division troops were still holding out, or maybe they were trapped, because behind the smoke which hid the river from the village came spasmodic bursts of automatic fire and the crump of mortar bombs.

The Indian gunners had taken up a position on the beach, firing their last gun while from the rest breech blocks and sights were removed and thrown down wells or into the river.

Bruce felt shattered. He felt nineteen, frightened and in despair. He had some fifty men to get across the river including the wounded, and he was the only swimmer. The sight of those desperate men down there, a great number of Gurkhas from other battalions among them who could not swim – indeed, from the looks of it, very few soldiers from any of the regiments could swim, or certainly not strongly enough to conquer the river. And especially now, it seemed from his observation point, that the tide had turned, speeding out to sea in the narrower section of the river just below the bridge, the current racing past the east bank. Every time a non-swimmer launched himself out onto the river on a makeshift raft, or clutching a length of bamboo, it was a leap into the dark, almost instantly coming to grips with the vicious current. How could he put his own men in such a dangerous, desperate situation? There must be some boats on the far bank.

'We will go back now.' Bruce said, trying with all his strength not to show the subedar how he felt. But he could sense Tilbir's fear, and the fear of the other Gurkhas, at the thought of what lay ahead.

Back with the rest of the company, Bruce said bluntly. 'We have seen what it is like, and it is not good. If we make rafts the chances are that not many will get across. I cannot lie about that – anyway, the Subedar Sahib has seen with his own eyes. The alternative might be to slip through the Jap lines, head east, then north and cross the river further upstream, although I fear that we have left it too late. We could, of course, surrender.'

'We cannot surrender.' The subedar shook his head violently. 'We would rather die fighting, or take a chance on the river. You, Sahib, must get across.'

'And leave you?'

'Perhaps you could get us started, give us some assistance in

132

the water. But you have the means to escape and must do so.'

'No, Sahib. Before I submit you to that devil's river, I must try and find a boat. I will swim across and search the far bank. The only difficulty might be in bringing it back alone, but we have nothing to lose, except time.'

'Then we will put our trust in you, Sahib.'

'Right. We will move forward and hide in the jungle near the river, on that cliff. It will soon be dark, and I think I would prefer to wait until then.'

'It shall be so, Sahib.'

They waited in the cover of the patchy jungle astride the cliff which overlooked the river. Darkness had come at last, but they could still hear the occasional shot, or a cry for help from a soldier drowning out in the river or wounded men waiting on the beach for someone who had promised to come back for them. And many a brave man did return. But it was a frustrating, despairing situation.

Bruce had no illusions as he lay on the ground. God, he thought, why did it have to come to this? How much more can men give of their courage, determination, belief in their commanders, pride in the traditions of their regiments? Must everything be a waste? All that marching and fighting come to an end on some stinking river in Burma because of other men's incompetence. Miles away from the front there were men who talked of a poor show by the troops in Burma – troops who had no experience of jungle warfare, pitched against an enemy numerically some three times greater and trained on the battlefields of China. But 17th Division had fought hard, and almost non-stop for five weeks, faced the enemy in close quarter combat, like the young Baluchis on the Salween who had held out for eight terrifying hours against heavy odds until by daylight the 7/10th Baluch Regiment had been practically annihilated and their colonel was among the dead.

All this was to delay the Jap advance and allow reinforcements to pour into Rangoon. Only he damn well knew that there was not much to pour into Rangoon. A trickle at the best. And then they had tied General Smyth's hands behind his back, and by the time he was allowed to move his division to the Sittang it was already too late.

And that was why they waited here, why more than 3,000 men who deserved so much more had to pit their wits and their lives in a battle against a mile wide river with an enemy waiting to strike if they should lose.

'Sahib,' Gopiram was shaking him by the leg. 'Somebody comes, Sahib.'

There was a low murmur of voices, then a figure crawled towards Bruce in the near darkness. 'Corporal Steel, sir. 2nd KOYLI,' he said in a young voice with a Yorkshire accent. 'And two men from the Burma Rifles.'

'Just you?'

'Lost the rest of my unit, sir, or rather they lost me when we broke up to try and reach the river. Two companies of the battalion in the perimeter, sir, and the 8th Burma Rifles, some Gurkhas from the 3/7th and the remnants of the Dogras. We didn't get the order to withdraw, and held out for some time until the Colonel decided we had better move out as everyone else seemed to have done. It wasn't easy breaking off from the Japs, and in the darkness I got separated. Then I bumped into two Karens from the Burma Rifles. We were making for the river when we were challenged by your men. You about to cross the river, sir?'

Bruce explained the situation. Steel murmured, 'So you are about to nip across on your own to find a boat.'

'Can you swim?' Bruce asked.

'Yes, sir. Battalion champion once. And the two Karen lads say they live by a river and are like fish in the water. That's what they say.'

'So you're all right,' Bruce said. 'Going to swim across now?'

'That was the general idea, sir.'

'Then good luck to you.'

Steel was silent for a moment. 'I thought you'd ask me to help out with the boat,' he said at last to Bruce's surprise.

'Why, yes, it had struck my mind for a moment. But it wouldn't be fair. You have no connection with my battalion. And there's too much risk, really, as we don't know when the Japs will come down to the river.'

'At times like these we are all the same, sir.'

'Are you absolutely sure?' Bruce tried to keep the obvious sense of relief out of his voice.

'Oh yes, sir.'

'Thank you Corporal Steel. Now where are those Karens?'

The Karens were one of the Burmese tribes particularly friendly and loyal to the British. When these two came up Bruce asked if they spoke English. One of them replied. 'Little, Thakin. My name is Maung Gyi. My friend is called Tun Hla.'

Bruce explained the situation to Maung Gyi slowly and he caught the gist of it because he said, 'We find boats for you. Come with you now.'

The four of them crawled out of the jungle patch and climbed down to the river's edge together with Tilbir, Gopiram and some riflemen. There was little movement on their section of the beach. By this time the other trapped soldiers had either crossed or drowned, or given up the attempt in favour of infiltrating north to seek another crossing point where they might find Burmese boats. Some managed to cross via the bridge, the Japs having abandoned the bridgehead, by means of a rope life-line stretched across the gap left by the demolition.

As Bruce and his swimmers stripped to their underpants, Steel said, 'Take your boots, sir. Round your neck by the bootlaces. If we have to scramble about looking for boats no knowing what creepy-crawlies may be around or sharp thorns.'

'Yes, good idea,' Bruce acknowledged.

The swimmers left their clothes with the beach party who would remain at the river's edge. The rest of the company would wait in the jungle with Thandraj in charge.

'We will try our best,' Bruce said to Tilbir.

'If you do not find a boat, Sahib, do not come back.'

'What do you mean?'

'The battalion will have to be reformed. They will need officer sahibs like you.'

'They will need much finer men like you,' Bruce said. 'I will be back, one way or another.'

'Then may God go with you, Sahib. I know you will not fail us.' To Bruce's surprise Tilbir grabbed his hands and held them for a moment, passing a message of friendship and respect. Then Tilbir released Bruce's hands and was once more the solid, dependable company subedar.

Bruce stepped into the river with the others and they began swimming in pairs, Steel and Bruce forming one pair, the Karens the other, each man to keep an eye on his partner, and help if he suddenly found himself in difficulty. Behind them the sky was lit with dozens of fires that flickered about Mokpalin and beyond. Now and again came the sound of a shot, a burst of automatic. That was all. And ahead it was all darkness and quiet.

Ahead also lay the river's power, its fast current and forceful tide, rushing out to the estuary, seizing Bruce suddenly in its grip, determined to take him out to sea in its fatal embrace. He kicked furiously, fighting against its force, seeing the dark mass of the shore rushing past, his arms beginning to ache as he kept up an overarm stroke. He thought he had broken through when he heard Steel cry out. The corporal swept past, twisting over in the current in his attempt to fight it but not succeeding. All Bruce's nerve ends were screaming at him to leave Steel alone. He was through the current, could make for the far shore. But he couldn't do it. He let himself be taken by the current and tide, adding speed with a swimming stroke.

He caught Steel, wondering for a horrible moment if the corporal was going to fight in a panic but he remained calm which took a lot of courage. Bruce started to take the strain as he pulled out of the current, Steel kicking his feet to help. The pressure on Bruce's arms seemed to be strong enough to wrench them out of their sockets. Then he felt as though he were being strangled, and realized that the bloody boots were trying to twist round his neck. He managed to get them over his head and let them sink into the vast depths of the river. He did the same with Steel's boots, and then the two men were able to move towards the far bank with more ease.

After what seemed an eternity, Bruce's feet touched the river bottom. Both men struggled to the bank and climbed up onto the shore where Steel collapsed. Bruce sat down, feeling the ground and the sky whirling like a merry-go-round. Gradually the sensation stopped and he was able to stand up and take stock of his surroundings. Westwards from the bank the ground seemed to be a vast stretch of open fields, while north and south there were the dark patches of trees and lengths of open bank. He wondered how far south the current had brought them. And what time it was. They must have been in the water for well over an hour, he calculated.

Steel was sitting up, his breath coming in deep gasps. 'Any better?' Bruce asked.

'Yes, sir. Thanks – I'm sorry about that. I thought I could swim the river without any trouble. Can't understand it.'

'The last few days have been pretty hard,' Bruce said. 'Sapped more of our energy than we realized, I suppose.' But he wondered if Steel really had been a swimming champion, or if he had only said that to make sure somebody would be on hand to help him across the river? It was too late to wonder why; they must move on and find a boat.

'We'll go northward,' Bruce said. 'Can't waste any more time.'

'I'm OK, sir,' Steel assured him.

They walked along the bank, the absence of boots making itself known at once as stones and grit cut their feet. But they struggled on, cursing, not making very good progress until luckily hitting a footpath when they were able to move along quickly. They kept looking out for any signs of boats, but there was only the naked shore. There was no sign of the Karens either; probably came ashore much further north, Bruce decided.

They covered another mile, reaching a thick clump of trees with jungle spreading out behind it and westwards. As they came under its dark, ominous cloak, Bruce could see the outline of a small creek. His heart was thumping as they approached, and then he saw what looked like the outline of a boat. And as he got nearer, eyes accustomed to the dark, he saw that it was a boat, pulled half way out of the creek, a big sampan, with a bamboo cabin built up in the middle. It looked in good order, and would carry around twenty passengers, he guessed.

But what was it doing there? They halted behind a tree, searching the area carefully, suspecting a trap. After about ten minutes, Bruce decided to go up to the boat. Steel reached it first and jumped aboard to look inside the bamboo cabin. And as Bruce hurried forward, Steel held up a couple of paddles. Thank God for that, Bruce thought.

Steel rejoined Bruce on the bank, and they put their

shoulders to the boat. It seemed as though it would never move, and they had to use much force before it began to slide down the bank, slowly at first, then with a sudden rush into the water. Steel climbed aboard and brought the boat alongside.

Bruce stood on the bank for a moment, hands on hips, getting his breath back. Then the night was split by the heavy rattle of a tommy-gun, and bullets spattered the dusty ground near his feet. He whirled round, horrified, to face a man who had come silently out of the darker jungle. He was obviously Burmese, wearing a *longyi*, the Burmese waistcloth, and a shirt of sorts. Bruce felt sick. All this way, Jap bayonets, shells, mortars and then to end up at the hands of a bloody Burmese bandit.

The *dacoit* shouted to someone still in the jungle; and as the man turned his head slightly to do so, in that instant Bruce felt the wind of something flashing past his face, heard the thump of a knife entering the *dacoit's* throat. The man dropped the tommy-gun, his hands grasping at the knife handle, trying to withdraw it.

Bruce ran forward, picked up the tommy-gun. The *dacoit* was on the ground, rolling over in his death agony. Bruce pulled out the knife, then rushed to the side of the boat. Steel took the knife and returned it to the leather sheath he had strapped on beneath his underpants.

'Quick, sir! He'll have mates, I'm sure.'

There were shouts in the jungle and two figures appeared. Bruce fired a burst, the leading man fell, the other turned, another burst and he clutched his side before stumbling into the undergrowth.

'Come on, sir!'

Bruce jumped into the boat which swayed for a moment then righted itself, and they paddled furiously out of the creek and onto the vastness of the river. Now the big boat was difficult to handle, caught in the current, trying to move sideways, while Bruce and Steel fought to keep it on a straight course, their arms aching from the unaccustomed application. By the time the boat grounded on the east bank their dried-out bodies were wet again with sweat. But by sheer luck, rather than skill, the boat had reached the shore below the cliff.

138

There were shadowy figures on the beach, but Tilbir's voice assured Bruce that all was well. 'How long do we have till daybreak?' Bruce asked him.

'About four hours, Sahib.'

'Then let us not waste time. Get the men down to the beach.'

'They are on their way. We caught a glimpse of the boat earlier, and I gave the order.'

'How were you so sure it was us?'

'Who else could it have been, Sahib?'

Bruce was overcome by this simple faith, and said roughly, 'Well, we must establish a strong bridgehead on the other side because there are *dacoits* in the area. Thandraj will go in the first detail to take charge, and the eight wounded.'

'Regretfully, two have died. One from 15 Platoon, the other a British soldier.'

'All right, the six wounded. I want to take as many of them across in the first trip. Only I am not sure how many the boat will carry.'

'There is only one boat, Sahib? I do not see the Karens.'

'They probably made good their escape,' Bruce said bitterly.

A moment later the rest of the company arrived on the beach. 'Dismantle the bamboo cabin,' Bruce ordered. 'We should then have more room for the stretcher cases.' And when this had been done, Bruce started loading the boat. Three of the wounded were taken aboard. Then, with some difficulty, Thandraj and four riflemen were squeezed in. Bruce had just sent up a silent prayer that the boat was not overloaded, when Tilbir caught his arm – something he would never have done in normal circumstances – and revealed the anxiety in his own mind.

'Another boat, Sahib.'

Bruce felt himself trembling in suspense until the boat came alongside. 'Thakin, Thakin! We lost you on the swim over,' Maung Gyi said. 'Then much trouble finding boat.'

Bruce felt guilty at his earlier conviction that the Karens had deserted. 'But you did find one, very well done, Maung Gyi.'

The Karen boat was loaded with the remainder of the stretcher cases; and five more of Thandraj's platoon. But as

Bruce was about to clamber into his boat, Maung Gyi said, 'Thakin. Rowing boat with many men too bad for you not being expert. Lose much time. You go with Tun Hla, and I take the other boat with the Corporal Thakin.'

Bruce agreed at once. And when the boats shoved off he was thankful that he had done so. Steel and he would have had great difficulty in controlling a heavily loaded craft. The skilful Karens, born to the task, cut the journey time by a good half, bringing the boats smoothly to rest on the west bank, a bit further south of the creek.

Thandraj and his men disembarked quickly to organize a bridgehead. Then the wounded were carried ashore, the company's little Gurkha medical orderly fussing over them.

The second trip was made in good time; now only Tilbir and one more platoon remained to be lifted off the east bank. Bruce and Steel were feeling the strain after the strenuous swim and the unaccustomed paddling, but the last trip was essential and daybreak was not far. Thankfully the Karens seemed hardly out of breath.

As the boats set out on the third journey, a faint glow was touching the jungle-covered hills beyond the eastern shore. The figures on the beach began to stand out quite clearly as daylight slipped rapidly over the far hills and spread down towards the river. Machine-gun fire suddenly chattered towards the direction of the bridge, and some rifle fire, then silence. The Japs must be closing on the river to see what pickings they could find; and Tilbir was organising his men in a defensive position. The boatmen pulled furiously; to Bruce the shore seemed so close and yet so far.

And then they were there. The Gurkhas running across the beach, loading quickly into the boats but in orderly fashion. In a matter of seconds the boats were pulling out, the east bank beginning to recede, and Bruce thought they had made it. But the unmistakable figures of Jap soldiers suddenly appeared on the beach, and rifle shots whined overhead. Two Japs were running forward with a machine-gun and setting it up.

The first burst of machine-gun fire snapped overhead, the next ricocheted off the water like stones from a boy playing ducks and drakes, only these missiles were more lethal than stones, and Bruce expecting another burst still had to concentrate on paddling steadily.

But Tilbir seized a Bren and opened fire from the stern, a second gunner and some riflemen joining him from the other boat. The bullets must have passed like hornets around the Jap machine-gunner's head because his next burst was wild, well away from the boats. But a rifle shot found a target, a Gurkha collapsing into the bottom of Bruce's boat with just one, deep sigh escaping his lips.

It was the last shot from the Japs. The subedar, who had a reputation as a marksman, found out the Jap machine-gunner and his number two, and they spilled their life-blood on a shore which had already seen too much death. The remaining Japs scurried away to safety.

Bruce could not help feeling sad for the little Gurkha who lay dead at the bottom of the boat. Only one bullet on target and he had to stop it. Why him? There was only one answer Bruce thought as they brought the boat alongside the west bank – it was the lottery of war.

Every bullet had somebody's name on it, so Bruce had been told enough times. But which one had his? He shook his head to clear his mind. He must move his men away from the river, and on to rejoin the rest of the division. There would be plenty of time to work it all out later – the war stretched a long way ahead. . .